LAD
ULT

LAD
ULT

NAVIGATING SAFELY FROM BOY TO MAN

DR. ANDY COPE & OLIVER COPE

CAPSTONE
A Wiley Brand

This edition first published 2026

Registered Offices
John Wiley & Sons, Inc., 111 River Street, Hoboken, NJ 07030, USA
John Wiley & Sons Ltd, New Era House, 8 Oldlands Way, Bognor Regis, West Sussex, PO22 9NQ, UK

For details of our global editorial offices, customer services, and more information about Wiley products visit us at www.wiley.com.

The manufacturer's authorized representative according to the EU General Product Safety Regulation is Wiley-VCH GmbH, Boschstr. 12, 69469 Weinheim, Germany, e-mail: Product_Safety@wiley.com.

Wiley also publishes its books in a variety of electronic formats and by print-on-demand. Some content that appears in standard print versions of this book may not be available in other formats.

Library of Congress Cataloging-in-Publication Data is Available:

ISBN 9781907326073 (Paperback)
ISBN 9781907326097 (ePDF)
ISBN 9781907326080 (ePub)

Cover Design and Image: Courtesy of Amy Bradley

Set in 10/14pt Frutiger LT Std by Straive, Chennai, India
Printed and bound by CPI Group (UK) Ltd, Croydon, CR0 4YY

C9781907326073_260825

Yes, it's a book for boys and young men, but we'd like to dedicate it to the important females in our lives.

We're shaped and completed by you.

With love and thanks.

Contents

About the Authors

It's highly unusual to have a father and son writing team so we'd better explain.

Dr Andy Cope is the proper grown-up one. He runs a training company and is lucky to work with some big name companies including Microsoft, Cadbury's, UEFA, SKY, Three and Astra Zeneca. He squeezes a book-writing career in among all that. Andy's writing journey started with children's fiction (his *Spy Dog* series has sold a million copies across the world) before doing a career U-turn.

His change of direction came as a result of gaining a PhD in positive psychology and becoming the UK's first ever 'Dr of Happiness'. In a nutshell, his job is to seek out happy people, study them, work out why they feel so amazing and share the ideas with a wider audience.

Andy pops up on radio, TV and podcasts. His aim is to change the emphasis from what's *wrong* with you to what's *right* with you. This book is special because, way back, he used to be a boy, then a young man, and is now a middle-aged man. Experience matters.

Ollie Cope is busy juggling work and studying. Ollie is *almost* a doctor. He is currently completing a university thesis that examines the link between social media and attention spans and when he qualifies, he'll be a 'Dr of Social Media'.

This is Ollie's first ever book. He brings the massive advantage of still being a young man and therefore in touch with how modern teenagers think and behave.

Combined, we bring youth and wisdom, light and dark, poker-faced and fun. We are seriously excited to have you on board.

Happy reading!

Andy & Ollie
andy@artofbrilliance.co.uk
ollie@artofbrilliance.co.uk

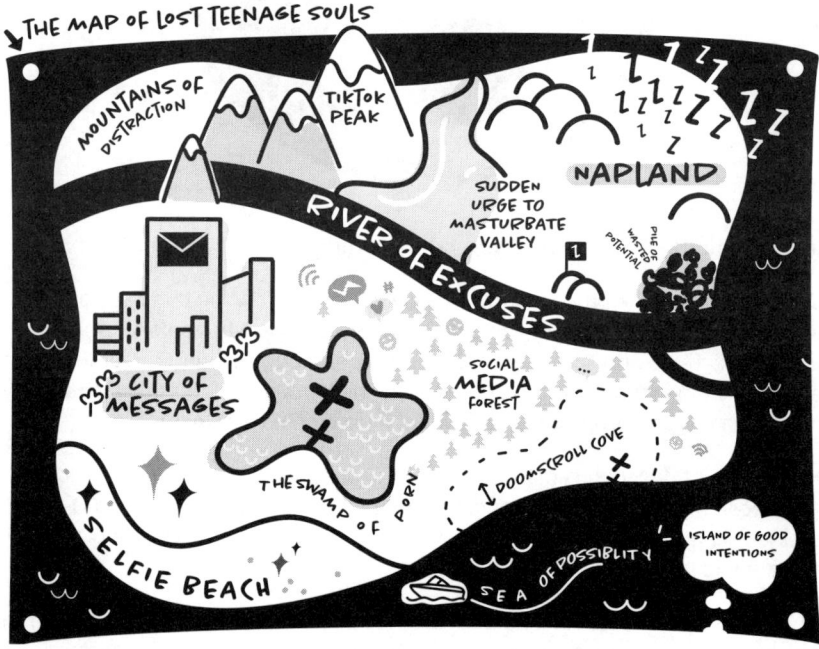

Pre-read Checklist

For the best experience we recommend *LADULT* is read old school, a chapter a night, preferably in bed. Failing that, your favourite chair. If neither are available, the toilet is quiet, comfy and (hopefully) undisturbed.

Before your turn the page please ensure you have:

✓ *'Who bought me this? I don't even like books'* mode, off'
✓ Your mind switched to 'open'
✓ Willingness to take action set to 'very'
✓ Your sense of humour turned up to 'max'
✓ Learning mode fully engaged
✓ Yellow highlighter for the really good bits
✓ Likelihood to leave five-star review set to 'highly'
✓ Mug of favourite beverage (biscuit, optional)
✓ All electronic devices turned off. Guessing that's not going to happen, so face down at least

Two important points before the off. First, it's important that you know *LADULT* contains a whole load of new information. New to you, and freshly created by your father-and-son writing team. It also contains some sections that are borrowed from Andy's other books – ideas that are so important that we've re-positioned them for young men.

Second, at no point are we going to tell you what to do. Our aim is to inform and entertain. Fingers crossed you enjoy the messages and, where necessary, are prodded into positive action. But, hey, that bit's up to you.

Thank you.

Chapter 1

A MAN DEFINED

Chapter Summary

Our puddle jumping, cartwheeling opener asks when you last ate a worm. Then it's a numbers game where we reveal the unfairness of life before attempting to define what you actually are – a man in the making. Then to the really tricky bit: what exactly is a 'man'? We get there via algae, angler fish and you'll be very grateful that you're *not* a Praying Mantis.

We introduce the concept of toxic masculinity, what it is, where it stems from and how to be the opposite. You'll learn about Dutch Disease and redefine 'cool' before moving on to some advice from the insect world. Plot spoiler: think like a bee and behave like a caterpillar – *eat great food, sleep a lot, wake up beautiful.*

It's worth hanging around for our chapter ending. Gilbert the alien, he's a joy.

But first, get revved up for something fast and furious.

Pit stop

Formula One is where the fastest drivers race the fastest cars in the world. To win an F1 race, you have to be faster and more furious than the other drivers. It's foot down, pedal to the metal all the way.

Except it isn't. *Not quite.*

The winning driver needs to come in for a couple of pit stops along the way. This is a chance to pull over, handbrake on, change tyres, refuel and get back in the race. The pit stops are crucial. If the driver fails to come in for a pit stop not only will he not win the race, he won't finish it.

You're so busy racing through life, navigating the day-to-day challenges of being a young man that you never get time out to reflect on your race strategy. *LADULT* is your pit stop. Press pause. Thinking time, refuelling your motivation and installing new habits before you re-enter the race of life.

But the Formula One analogy falls a little flat because F1 is full of glamour, wealth, exotic locations and sexy people, whereas most people's lives are a bit more bland. A more realistic analogy might be Mario Kart. Navigating through teenage growing pains has always been hazardous. Adolescence is a time of intense changes to your body, a ramping up of emotions as well as significant banana skins in your social world. Factor in the Mario Kart oil slicks of AI, neurodiversity, social media, terminally online 'brain rot' and easy access to porn, and you can find yourself spinning out of control.

So it's worth silently congratulating yourself for getting this far! You're on the Mario Kart grid. Our job is to get you ready for the craziness.

The point of *LADULT* is that you're a man-in-the-making, a male with L-plates. The book will help you sift through the excess of information there is about being a man and to help you make up your own mind about what kind of man you want to become.

That sentence is more important than it sounds because it points to potential pathways and choices that shape your future.

If you're already bursting with energy, brimming with confidence and have a backbone of steel, congrats. If you're acing school, have a dream job lined up, have hatched a plan to woo your perfect partner, have already chosen names for your three amazing children to be and have an unshakeable belief that you're going to nail an epic life, go you! You can skip *LADULT*. You have our permission to pass it on to someone else or leave it in the bathroom so your family can absorb the messages.

If, on the other hand, you need the cheat codes, then this book will race you through a few levels. We're unashamedly pitching in at 'best life' territory. Which, by spooky coincidence, starts by crafting your 'best self'.

The question is, how? How the heck am I supposed to 'live my best life' and 'be my best self' when the world's throwing so much at me?

It's a fair question because it's mightily easy to NOT show up in life as your best self. There are a lot of people talking a good talk and curating a virtual version of 'living the dream', but if you scratch the surface, it's a nightmare. There's a lot of smoke and mirrors. Too many people are living a 'karaoke life' where they're singing along to a song sheet written by somebody else.

As a teenager, you might have already noticed the magic withering away. Think of any under-five kid you know. Guaranteed they're skipping, puddle-splashing, duck-chasing, story-listening, hand-holding, cartwheeling, worm-eating, sandcastle-building whirlwinds of energy, curiosity and fun. Just like you used to be.

Now think of any over 35 you know. When was the last time they jumped in a puddle, chased a duck or cartwheeled in the park?

Exactly!

Thought for the day

'Can you remember who you were, before the world told you who you should be?'

Charles Bukowski (American writer)

During our teenage years, we get the magic educated right out of us. We learn to fit into what society thinks we should be. You can feel like a square peg in a society of pre-drilled round holes. We learn that life comes in phases – born, nursery, school, college, work, consume, retire, die – and if all goes according to plan there should be some brief interludes of happiness along the way.

Here's the problem with adults; they dish out a lot of advice that might or might not have worked for them 'back in the day'. Our argument is that those days are gone.

Your days are different – radically faster, more pressurised and full-on than whenever 'back in the day' was.

Wakey-wakey

Change doesn't start with action. Don't get me wrong, we need to take action along the way but that's not where change starts. Deep, lasting change starts with us waking up and seeing things in a way that we didn't see before. Action follows from there.

It's a tap on the shoulder. Wakey-wakey. There's no learning, figuring out or action without that tap on the shoulder.

So here's your tap. Your wake-up call, delivered by some important numbers.

LAD FACT

Infinity is a concept, not a number. In actual fact, Graham's number is the biggest number in the world. It's mindbogglingly immense. Graham's number is so big that if you wrote it down the numbers wouldn't fit into the observable universe.

The average UK human lifespan is 4,212 weeks. Women tend to get a few more (4316 as against ours, which is 4108. Chill, we have got a whole section on life not being fair coming up soon)

And whereas your average cat has nine lives, humans tend to just get one. Again, not fair but life is what it is, a one-time only special offer.

This book is about the 4,000 or so weeks that the average human spends breathing.

That's 4,000 Mondays (*boo-hiss!*)

And 4,000 Saturdays (*woo-hoo!*)

Which, straight away, gets to the nub of the problem: social learning!

Usually, by age 10, young people have learned that Mondays are bad and Saturdays are good. It's not formal learning. Nobody sits you down and explains it, but you look around at your teachers and parents and they seem to be a bit zombified on Monday, then, as the week progresses, they gradually spark into life, reaching full bloom at

**SMONDAY
The moment
when Sunday
stops feeling like
a Sunday and the
anxiety of Monday
starts to kick in.**

about 4 pm on Friday. Saturdays are epic. Sundays too, until about 7 pm when the 'Smonday' feeling kicks in.

If literally *everyone* thinks Mondays are rubbish and literally *everyone* wakes up to the magnificence of life on Friday afternoon, guess what, it's easy to start doing the same.

We learn by watching others.[1] Human beings are the world's greatest fitter-inners.

But here's the twist – if you want to have an amazing life you're best off looking around at what everyone else is doing and NOT DOING THAT! Instead of being a fitter-inner, you need to learn to be a stander-outer.

Which is such a simple idea but really hard to execute in real life. To stand out you'd have to go against conventional wisdom and challenge yourself to do everything a bit better than you have to. That means being kinder than you have to, working harder than you have to, being more polite than you have to, listening better than you have to, doing your homework a bit better than you have to. . .

It makes perfect logical sense because it's so obvious – over time, all these tiny changes would build up to a whopper of a difference. While everyone else is doing 'just enough' your 'do it better than I have to' mantra means you will power ahead.

This is a great theory until you factor in the teenage virus 'can't be botheredness'. It's like flu, in that males catch it much worse than females. All this 'best life', 'do extra', 'be better' can sound like *blah blah blah. Yes, I get it, but I'll start tomorrow or next week or next year.*

The bare-knuckled truth? You are living your one precious life. No rehearsals. No do-overs. No re-spawning.

This is it!

Your potential is one thing. What you do with it is quite another.

LAD FACT

Tomorrow is a concept, created in the mind. It is a thought. Nobody actually lives there. In fact, nobody has ever visited tomorrow. Deciding to take action tomorrow means you're opting for no action.

Good news – someone loves you enough to have bought this book for you. You can repay them three times over. First, with a genuine thank you. Second, by reading it cover to cover. Third, by taking positive action as a result of what you've read.

They bought *LADULT* because they want you to have an amazing life which is great but not enough. *You* have to want it too.

But, hey, the modern world has added extra layers of complexity, so before we *properly* begin, we have to dive into the thorny issue of what even is a man?

What's your MAN-ifesto?

A brief word

Something we need to make clear is that this book is for *all* young men. The book will mention relationships and sometimes we will talk about relationships with the opposite sex. But we are well aware that some of you reading this book may not be interested in girls, at least not in *that* way. We want you to know that this book is for you too, because whoever you are attracted to has no bearing on our message. We know that all young men can benefit from reading this book because all young men, whatever their preference, can fall victim to the curse of mediocrity and toxicity.

Becoming a wonderful human being is independent of who you fancy.

To those of you to whom this applies, you might sometimes face challenges that heterosexual people won't face. This is completely unfair, and we're sorry if this happens to you, but it's why we think *LADULT* is vital for you.

It'll help you thrive when you encounter those who carry the bigotry gene.

Opinions have always existed. Theories too. Oh, and idiots have been around forever.

Back in the day, you were free to share your views with your closest few. Then communication went viral and nowadays everyone can share their opinions with millions of people across the world. Experts have a platform, wise people have a voice but so do idiots and rabble rousers. Theories morph into conspiracies. The debate can get loud, toxic and downright confusing.

Some of the debate is useful: Is eating bread good or bad for you? Is global warming real? Do we actually need democracy? Is social media damaging? And some less so: Is the earth flat? Are big data companies using our personal information to fulfil their grand scheme where the global elites enslave us all with a mind virus and turn us into brain mush puppets who will do nothing but consume to our heart's content while they feed on endangered animals and bathe in virgins' blood?

Hard to tell. Depends on whom you listen to.

This ability to hear extreme opinions on any subject means that we are struggling to come to a consensus on anything,[2] including things that used to be rock solid such as the definition of a *man* (or indeed a *woman*).

Which begs the question, what does the word 'man' mean to you?

It is a word that conjures up different things for different people. Some may think of physical strength, deep voice, a square jaw and a traditional 'real man' occupation that requires them to wear a high viz jacket and hard hat. Others may think of oppression and toxicity. To some it is a hard biological fact, something you either are or are not, to others it is a purely social category that can be floated in and out of at will.[3]

The fluidity of the modern definition matches the slipperiness of the experience of being a male of the species. Men's role in society is increasingly being questioned, with some people stating that men need to 'change' whereas others claim that men need to 'keep being men more than ever'.[4] On the one hand we learn that 'real men don't cry' and, on the other, that 'modern men should express their emotions'. Teenage boys can get caught up in all this swirling debate. It's head-scratchingly confusing – are we supposed to 'man up' or 'man down'?

To untangle some of the confusion, let's rewind to a couple of billion years ago when everything was a lot less complicated. In fact, 'life' back then couldn't have been simpler, mostly consisting of micro-organisms like algae. They reproduced asexually, meaning that they could have 'babies' without the input of another organism, and it would often occur under times of stress.[5] Imagine going back to these 'good old days' – you're feeling a bit stressed about an exam and BOOM – you spontaneously clone yourself.

At some point between one and two billion years ago, 'sexual reproduction' emerged. All sexual reproduction actually means is just the mixing of the genetics of two members of the same species to create unique offspring. Eventually, although we aren't exactly sure when, this led to some species having two distinct members. These were ones that carried sperm and ones that carried eggs. Or, as we would go on to call them, males and females.[6]

In *most* species of animals on earth, males and females are different. This includes humans.

When we say males and females, we do not mean what individuals identify as; we are talking about *biological* sex. Males and females of species being different is something called *sexual dimorphism*, and it's something that varies between many species on earth.[7] In some species there are only small differences between the males and females, whereas in others there are very extreme differences.

One very extreme example is the deep-sea angler fish, which is the scary fish with a lamp on its head as seen in *Finding Nemo*. Female angler fish are the ones we are used to seeing, with the scary teeth and the headlamp, whereas the male angler fish are tiny, way smaller than the females. The weirdest part is that when the angler fish mate, the tiny male latches on to the female and permanently fuses to her body like a parasite, gaining nutrients from her in exchange for providing sperm. . . how romantic. This weird relationship occurs because of the extreme pitch-black deep-sea environment that the angler fish live in. It's a crazy example but it goes to show how males and females can be *vastly* different.[8]

LAD FACT

However tough things might seem for the modern male, consider yourself lucky that you're not a Praying Mantis. Famously, in the mantis community, the female eats the male, often during or before sexual intercourse. Yes, you read that correctly – *'before'* – headless lovemaking is a thing in the mantis community.[9]

We'll spare you the gory boyish details; suffice it to say that the act of Mantis lovemaking is often his final act. No wonder they're called *Praying* Mantis! *'If there's a God up there, Dear Lord, please don't let her chew my head off.'*

Humans are sexually dimorphic, but thankfully not as significantly as the angler fish. Female humans mature earlier than males, which is why early in secondary school most of the girls are taller than you, as well as going through menstruation once a month. Adult human males usually have deeper voices and grow more facial/body hair, and on average are bigger and stronger than females. The key here is that I say *on average*. There are some very impressive female athletes out there who can out bench-press me by a mile. But *on average* a woman's strength is between 60% and 80% of that of a man's, with men having a particular advantage in the upper body. Adult males tend to be taller, have more muscle mass, stronger bones, larger lungs/heart, and better designed joints for athleticism than women.[10] This is why most sports are divided into genders because it's not a level playing field in terms of strength and speed.[11]

Throughout human history, males and females have played to their natural strengths.

It's commonly believed that when we lived in tribal societies (100,000+ years ago) it made sense to harness men's strength and speed and send them to hunt *large* animals (although women would still hunt smaller animals and find other foods), and that the men would be the ones who fought in conflicts against other tribes.[12]

Women had more of a child-rearing role, particularly with younger children. For thousands of years this was just the way it was. The difference between men and women, male and female, was written into their world. For a lot of human history, laws and rules have been written *by* men and *for* men. Women have generally been much more restricted in the things they were allowed to do or even to say. Women were forbidden for centuries from participating in politics and were also banned from doing many of the same activities as men, such as going to school or playing sports. It was even considered 'unwomanly' to read too much![13]

Understandably, many women were not happy with this arrangement and, thankfully, the first wave of feminism opened up women's right to vote in the UK in 1928. Education changed, legislation gave women equal rights, and we are where we are today. We can look around at parts of the world where women haven't got the same rights and freedoms, and think of ourselves as incredibly fortunate to be living in a fair society. (Note, fair doesn't mean perfect. We still have some way to go).

In many areas women haven't just caught up, they've overtaken us! For example, girls are now 35% more likely to go to university than boys.[14] This means that the old dynamic of the man going out to earn the money while the woman stays at home to look after the family is pretty old school.

With women now not *needing* men to have money, be successful or even to raise children, the role of men has become less well defined. Which brings us full circle to the question that kicked off this section: *what does the word 'man' mean to you?*

Beware of Dutch disease

Most people are lovely. But a small minority of males and females are toxic. There is actually something called 'toxic femininity' but it tends not to hit the headlines like its male equivalent. Toxic masculinity is a phrase that's cloaked in confusion, so let's unmask it for you.

As the name implies, it's positioned at the poisonous end of manliness. It's linked with misogyny (dislike, disrespect or prejudice against women) and the need to dominate by force.[15]

It's definitely to be avoided. But some of the swirling confusion arises from those with loud social media voices. The shouty people have claimed that men who exercise are being toxic, that video games cause toxic masculinity, sitting with your legs apart ('manspreading') is toxic, and that liking team sports is a toxic masculine trait. At the extreme end of the argument, men are labelled as 'toxic' just for being men.

Let's draw a line in the sand here. Yes, toxic masculinity *does* exist but it *isn't* toxic to exercise, play games or to like competitive sports. Oh, and 'manspreading' isn't an act of sexist dominance, merely a comfortable way to sit when you've got a set of balls between your legs.[16] That said, sitting *uncomfortably* with your legs crossed to give other people room is a polite thing to do.

Genuine toxic masculinity exists in the form of those guys who always need to prove something by force. You'll wince when you see it. The guy that can't take any criticism without throwing a tantrum, who always feels the need to pick on someone whom he sees as an easy target, who goes out of their way to harass girls, who takes banter way too far, and who always has to have 'their way'.

The toxics make other people feel bad about themselves so that they can feel better about *themselves*. You have to admit that having a desire to make other people feel low is pretty low in and of itself.

So where does this come from? How come some men end up being toxic but others don't? The simple truth is that it's a coping mechanism that often stems from a lack of confidence.[17] Someone who is *not* confident talking to girls will resort to being mean to them to hide their nerves; someone who is *not* confident in themselves will resort to putting others down to make themselves feel better; someone who is *not* confident won't be able to take jokes or criticism because they're unsure of themselves.

Which points to a big 'what if?'

Rather than men being toxic by nature, what if it's just that there are too many men who are lacking in confidence? For some men, life is one big contest of showing how cool they are and in the mad scramble to be top dog, their masculine poison bubbles to the surface.

So hang in there for some big thoughts, via the Netherlands . . .

There is a concept in economics (stay with me) known as Dutch disease. The idea is that if a country's economy relies too much on making money from one thing, then the country is asking for trouble. It's called Dutch disease because it happened in the Netherlands, where the discovery of a huge field of natural gas caused other industries in the country to decline.[18]

Putting all of your eggs into an unreliable basket can happen to entire nations but it can also happen to personal confidence.

If you're always relying on the outside world for your confidence, then you're essentially gambling with your wellbeing. Think about it – if you rely on others to feel confident but other people don't give you what you need, then all of a sudden your confidence is way down, and this might lead to some toxic behaviour to try to make yourself feel better (maybe by picking on someone or by lashing out).

Of course, it's nice to get reassurance and approval from people whose opinions about us really matter, but we shouldn't be *relying* on it. The key to real confidence is realising that it comes from within. Confidence is boosted if you have self-belief that you are becoming a better person. It doesn't happen overnight; confidence comes bit by bit, day by day, and being able to answer (honestly), *am I a better human than I was yesterday?*

There will be some backward steps but if the answer is 'yes' more often than 'no', you're heading in the right direction. It's important to understand that the non-toxic path is much more rewarding. You can choose to nourish rather than poison.

You're not a better person because you were the alpha male in the room or because you imposed yourself on others, but because you were someone who was a total pleasure to be around.

You're not a better person because you tore someone down, but because you lifted the people around you.

You're not a better person by being the loudest but sometimes by remaining strongly silent.

You're not a better person by joining the wrong crowd but by walking away from it.

You're not a better person by answering back but by showing respect.

You get the point. Being a non-toxic man doesn't mean you are passive. You can still stand up for what is right and for what you believe in; you can be a leader through positive example and encouragement rather than through force. You can still be fun and make rude/brutal jokes with your friends, but without crossing the line into unnecessary abuse or bullying. You can still be admired, but for your real achievements that mean something rather than the ones you post online.

It boils down to this: self-confidence and self-esteem should have SELF in capitals! If you have high self-esteem and you walk around knowing that you're valued, loved and worthy, then you won't feel the need to tear anyone else down to make yourself feel better.

How to improve your likeability

'Narcissism' is a big word that's got a long history. It's being talked about because it's becoming more common, so what is it?

Back story. . . Narcissus was a very handsome young man from Greek mythology. As the story goes, one day he was wandering in the woods and discovered a pond. Narcissus leant down for a drink, saw his own reflection and fell in love with himself. Plot spoiler, it didn't end well for the lad. He died and his name lives on, but not in a good way. Narcissists are people who are preoccupied with themselves. They are self-centred, selfish and lack empathy.

Younger children tend to go through a phase that borders on narcissism. A toddler has to learn to share, empathise and master all the caring and listening skills that are required to be a good friend. Except, once again, today's 'selfie culture' conspires to push you the wrong way. 'Self-love' is all well and good, but it can go too far. Posting endless selfies, chasing followers instead of friends, being overly interested in yourself, thinking you're the bee's knees, talking about yourself all the time.

A word of warning. Please don't become that *me-me-me-me-me* person.

By all means respect yourself, like yourself, be kind to yourself and talk nicely to yourself, but don't fall head over heels in love with yourself. It didn't end well for Narcissus and it wouldn't end well for you. Narcissistic adults tend to be attention-seeking, arrogant and difficult to love.

Rather than 'selfie', it pays to be 'othery' because here's the number one thing that shoots you to the top of the popularity stakes, and it's probably not what you imagine. Being popular is less about confidence, intelligence, good looks or charm. For people to like you, it helps to like them first. If everyone in your class writes down a list of people they like, the key to your likeability is that the list of 'who you like' is longer. Of course, your list has to be genuine. You actually have to like people and, if you do, you become genuinely interested in them and, in a bizarre twist of the universe, they will also like you.[19]

Obviously, you don't have to like everybody and not everyone has to like you. There will always be a couple of unlikeable jerks, but if you can see the good in most people and become a person who likes others, you'll reap the benefit.

How to be cool

There's always a handful of people at school who seem to have got the memo on how to dress, act and, for the lack of a better word, be 'cool'. There are others who were at the back of the queue when 'cool' was being handed out.

It's all too easy to fall into the trap of thinking that to be accepted, you need to conform to some arbitrary standard of what 'cool' is. You try and water yourself down, to hide your quirks and fit into a cookie-cutter shape that is not really you at all. The irony is that in many people's attempts to be 'cool' and 'stand out', they just end up becoming like everybody else because they're desperately trying to hide their uniqueness that makes them who they are.

Paranoia is a feeling that people are talking about you behind your back, most probably saying nasty things. But here's its wonderful opposite, *pronoia*, when people are saying nice things about you. Imagine, just for a second, that people are bigging you up behind your back.

Then imagine, just for another second, what kind of person you'd need to be for people to be saying amazing things about you when you're not in earshot. Teachers, parents, friends, classmates, lady next door, bus driver, bloke on the checkout, lunchtime supervisors, gran, sister, Aunty Kylie . . . what would you have to do to make all these people go 'Wow'?

This is about consistency and something we call 'trademark behaviours'. These two factors combine to build your reputation. We're not talking about being the typical popular kid at school. This is much more powerful than being the alpha male. We're talking about having character, compassion and connection that tell everyone else who you are and what you stand for. A lot of people believe that accumulating achievements, honours, medals or 'followers' is the only way to establish a solid reputation, whereas the reality is that a really exceptional reputation is built on the tiniest acts of kindness, the time spent listening, the support and encouragement you give and your willingness to help others. Consistency in these trademark behaviours marks you out as someone special.

We think it's worth redefining 'cool'. Being cool means knowing when to say 'no' when something doesn't seem right. It's about maintaining your values when others don't. It's having the courage to be nice in a society that occasionally glorifies cruelty. Cool is being the friend who makes sure everyone gets home safely after a party.

> **Be genuinely interested in other people**
>
> The next time you have a conversation with a friend or loved one, set your intention to listen with your full attention. Phone away, eye contact, interested face on, ears pinned back, mouth closed, tuned in – be genuinely interested in the human and they'll think you're amazing.
>
> Oh, and the best question you can ask to show you're interested is this: 'Tell me more . . .'

Caterpillar soup

Businessman Rory Sutherland points out an interesting fact about bees. There are a certain number of bees in every colony who will disobey the orders of the other bees. These 'maverick' bees don't follow the swarm.

They do their own thing, taking risks by flying into uncharted territory in search of new flowers. Scientists struggled to explain this for a while, but eventually they realised that if it weren't for these bees that broke the mould and acted differently from the crowd, the entire colony would die out when their usual flowers ran out of pollen.[20]

If you become a confident man who openly expresses his positive emotions, you will be like one of those maverick bees. You won't do what the crowd is doing, and a lot of people might not understand you, but we need you more than ever.

It's not toxicity, it's confidence. *Bee that man*.

Which reminds me, speaking of insects, here's one more thought.

The Very Hungry Caterpillar is one of the best kids' books ever. The clue's in the title but here's your plot spoiler . . . a caterpillar gets the munchies and scoffs its way through traditional caterpillar fare – pears and apples and plums – before progressing to cupcakes, sausages and cherry pie.

Taken literally, it's a powerful message about what happens if you eat too many cupcakes, sausages and cherry pies, although I'm not sure that's the point?

The twist for under-fives is that the caterpillar locks itself away in a chrysalis and shapeshifts into a beautiful butterfly.

What goes on inside the chrysalis is private. The story remains quiet as the caterpillar goes through an identity change. The book doesn't illustrate this bit because, I would imagine, kids would have nightmares. Inside the chrysalis, the grub's organs and tissue dissolve into some sort of caterpillar soup which then somehow reconstitutes itself into the body of a butterfly that bears no resemblance to a caterpillar at all. All throughout this pupa soup stage, the creature remains alive, with just enough strength left over to break out of the chrysalis, flap its amazing new wings and get eaten by a blackbird.

It's a radical shift of identity from chubby grub to winged butterfly.

How does it know?

It's what the French call 'élan vital', a life force or 'impulse of life' that every organism has. The cells have instructions. There's a plan. A template. And all the while that the struggle is going on inside the chrysalis, the process is reliant on external conditions. The weather, the rotation of the earth so the right amount of sunlight, the length of the days . . . there's a cosmic rhythm.

Ultimately, the successful metamorphosis depends partly on what's going on inside the chrysalis and partly on the conditions outside. We'll be looking at what's going on inside of you, but the next chapter focuses on the world out there and how it might be impacting on the life inside your head.

The invasion

Imagine you are at home, one eye on the game you're playing, the other eye on the view from your kitchen window. Suddenly, your jaw drops open and the controller smashes on the floor as you watch a spaceship land in your back garden. A hatch opens, some smoke billows out, and a small purple alien shuffles down a ramp. A few seconds later there's a soft knock at your door. You're frozen to the spot until a second knock brings you to your senses.

You open the door, just a crack and sure enough, the small purple creature is right there. It's about half the size of a human so you crouch down to eye level.

'Hi there. Have you c-c-c-come to take over planet earth? Are you here to k-k-kill the humans?'

'Gosh no,' beams the little creature. 'Whatever makes you think that? I'm Gilbert and I come in peace. But I need your help.'

The intergalactic traveller explains that it's from Planet Glee, where everyone is impossibly happy, all of the time. 'It's unbearable,' chuckles the small grape-like creature. 'We're literally laughing all day long, having sweet dreams, and then doing the same next day.'

I'm guessing you've got a surprised look on your face. Planet Glee sounds amazing, right? 'So why have you come knocking at my door?'

'Well,' smiles the alien, 'all this happiness and laughing is making our sides ache and we have a terrible incontinence problem'.

You gawp at Gilbert. 'You're wetting yourselves with laughter?'

'Oh gosh, yes,' chuckled the alien. 'And of course when someone wets their pants it's so funny that it sets off a chain reaction and before you know it your family's ankle deep. So we're interested in finding out about sadness and negativity. My people have sent me to earth on a fact-finding mission. I've got to find the secrets of grumbling and misery. What pointers can you give me? What can I do to lower my levels of happiness? I'm going to scribble your ideas down and take them back to Planet Glee. I'll be a hero because it'll end our incontinence problem, we won't have to walk around in wellies, and there will be no more aching sides. So, dear human, please tell me, how can I feel glum?'

What advice would you give to the alien?

Now go do the exact *opposite* of that!

Chapter 2

ALL ABOARD THE STRUGGLE BUS

Chapter Summary

Nowadays storms have names. The weather person tells us that 'Storm Benedict' is coming and we should all stay indoors because he's a bit gusty. If you're really lucky the storm closes the school and you have a sneaky Benedict day.

I have a feeling that Storm Benny's arrived, but in our heads. I think we're in the grip of extreme *mental* weather. This chapter looks at what's causing the grey clouds. We introduce the change-quake zone before being totally counter-intuitive and arguing that modern life might actually be too easy.

Moving swiftly through cognitive load theory we take a day trip to the zoo where the animals are behaving badly. In between the heavy content we find time for burnt toast, scary squirrels and hint that the world might be messing with our heads.

The change-quake era

Nobody's sure of the exact figure but the best guess is that over 100 billion humans have lived on planet earth and yet there's never been anyone quite like you.[21] Your DNA is unique. You are made of 37 trillion cells, each one containing the same DNA, the blueprint of you. Your height, eye colour, basic body shape, shoe size – you can thank your mum and dad – these are pre-programmed.

But the brand new science of epigenetics suggests the *sequencing* of your genes is dependent largely on your environment. Some of your genes can be switched on and off. That means you and the genes you pass on are moulded by experiences.[22] So let's take a look at the external environment and how it might be shaping us right now.

At some point you'll have watched a devastating news report about an earthquake. The tectonic plates will have rubbed up the wrong way, the earth shook, buildings collapsed and people got trapped in the rubble.

Earthquakes are measured on the Richter scale and because news only reports on big stuff, guaranteed it will have registered as a 7 or above.

Imagine, just for a second, that we used the Richter Scale to measure change. We think the modern world is a 9.5 or maybe a 9.6. The 'change' needle is all over the place.

People are being shaken up. If you look at the mental health statistics, it feels like we're standing in the rubble of mental health collapse. What's more, the aftershocks keep coming. Sometimes it can feel as though there's no recovery time between one wave of change and the next.

To be clear, humans have always found ways to adapt to change; it's just that throughout most of history change has been slow, allowing us to keep pace.

And then, all of a sudden, in the blink of an evolutionary eye, it wasn't slow!

In the business world they call it a VUCA environment (volatility, uncertainty, complexity and ambiguity). Your lifetime has seen change accelerate to warp speed. Climate emergency, migration, technology, social media, technology, algorithms, neurodiversity, gender fluidity, epidemics, pandemics, artificial intelligence, fake news, wars, influencers . . . in such bewildering times, it's no wonder that the world's reserves of happiness and wellbeing are running dangerously low.

Which brings us to a question: *what skills and qualities do we need if we're going to thrive in the change-quake era?* Note, the question doesn't say, what skills and qualities do we need to scrape by or survive – we deliberately used the word 'thrive'. Because, you see, there's a vast difference between 'surviving' and 'thriving'. One involves having a pulse; the other involves making it race a bit. Thriving raises the bar from 'getting through the week' to 'enjoying the week'. It's a massive about-turn, away from the masses who have learned to count down to Fridays, to someone who's head over heels in love with Mondays.

The problem isn't change per se, it's that we've accelerated from tortoise to cheetah.

Our point is that *thriving* in the change-quake era requires a different set of skills. Those old style 9–5 jobs still exist but are far less common. You're more likely to end up working at your kitchen table, which is kind of cool, except there's nobody to ask or to bounce ideas off. You need to be a problem solver. With the world moving at pace, you're going to need bags of resilience and a huge wedge of positivity. A sense of humour is helpful for when things don't go according to plan. The modern world requires you to be creative, to re-think a situation, to take a calculated risk, to dare to fail and to think on your feet. More than anything, you're going to need to be a lifelong learner and an opportunity creator.

We're not suggesting that change is bad. Pace brings a certain thrill. We're the only humans in history to have wi-fi, social media, music streaming, same day delivery, click and collect and a coffee shop on every street corner. We're comfortable. In fact, those of us in the developed world are living lifestyles as lavish as kings and queens of yesteryear.

The world has bent over backwards to give us what we thought we wanted – and yet it has somehow driven a wedge between us and our wellbeing .

So here's a super controversial thought – have we made everything too easy? No, hang in there, hear me out. For all of human eternity we've been struggling to eke out an existence. Way back, assuming you survived the ordeal of being born, old age was 30! Disease, starvation, drought, a battle with the village in the next valley – the aim has always been to get through the week. We fought tooth and nail just to stay alive.

And now life's handed to us on a plate. For ever (and ever and ever and ever), humans have died from scarcity. Not enough food, clean water, sanitation, medication, warmth or safety. For the entirety of human history, it's been a struggle to survive. Food has been so scarce that it´ was almost impossible to get fat.

And then WHAM, here you are, the first generation in human history to be dying from too much! The tables have been turned and all of a sudden it's very difficult to NOT be overweight. People are literally dropping dead from abundance! Yes, in a bizarre twist of evolution, obesity is killing more people than starvation.[23]

Our eyes are bigger than our bellies. We're like Oliver Twist who quite innocently asked, 'Please Sir, can I have some more?' and boy, did we get more! More calories, more stuff, more choice, more data, more followers, more speed, more pressure, more to do, more complexity, more to match up to, more to catch up with, more to compare with . . .

. . . more than we bargained for.

Welcome to the change-quake zone. This is your era, where the fight for physical health has been displaced by the battle for mental health. Remaining alive is easier, remaining sane less so. Because layered onto all of this is something that scientists call 'cognitive load theory'. Hang in there while we explain . . .

Ctrl-alt-delete

Truth be told, those pesky algorithms have moved faster than human evolution. Our brains are stuck in first gear as the algorithmic Lamborghini speeds into the distance.

But, of course, your brain doesn't want to be eating dust. It wants to keep up. So it works super hard, all the cogs are turning and the neurons firing at warp speed as we consume information. Duped by stimulating screen content, doped up on dopamine, that two pounds of grey matter between your ears is running red hot.

That's the context. It's not necessarily good or bad, it just is.

At home, when everyone's logged on and downloading something at the same time, the Wi-Fi is ultra slow and you get that round and round gizmo on your screen. Cognitive Load Theory is similar, but when your brain is buffering. When there's too much happening around you and not enough brainpower to process everything, your brain starts whirring round and round, and you're heading for trouble.[24]

Just as your wi-fi sometimes needs rebooting, so do you.

If we revved up a buzz saw and took off the top of your skull, there's a lot of complicated wiring in there. One of the issues is a good news/bad news problem.

The good news is that you have caution baked into your operating system. We all do. It's not something you can do a great deal about, other than recognise that's how *Homo sapiens* are manufactured. Psychologists call it negativity bias; it's why you remember criticism and forget a compliment.[25] An awareness of it helps you compensate for it.

Essentially, we didn't evolve for happiness. Happiness is nice to have but not crucial for survival. Primitive humans didn't sit around journalling or meditating; they were too busy clinging onto life by their fingernails. Our minds evolved to help us survive in a world fraught with physical danger. Imagine that you're an early human hunter-gatherer – covered in lice, wearing some sort of animal fur, no deodorant, terrible hair, in an environment full of bitey, stingy, poisonous, vicious predators. If you wanted to survive, you had to be vigilant. The absolute number one priority of the primitive human brain was to look out for anything that might harm you – and keep well away. Dr Evian Gordon calls it the 'fundamental organising principle of the brain', suggesting our senses scan the environment five times a second, looking for danger.[26]

Five times a second!

Basically, humans have an ultra-vigilant 'don't get killed' device, fitted as standard.

If your brain sniffs danger, it's programmed to assume the threat is real unless it can be proved otherwise. Caution is EVERYTHING! Why? Because back in the fur skin, campfire, spear-wielding days, the assumption of clear and present danger saved our bacon. We were programmed to flee from the rustle in the bushes *every single time*, even when it was only a squirrel. This 'better safe than sorry' safety mechanism means getting it wrong 1,000 times and fleeing from 1,000 squirrels is better than misjudging it once.

One miscalculation, *one* lapse, *one* moment of carelessness, *one* moment of letting your guard down – it's a bear rather than a squirrel – and you're a goner.

The world has moved on but our brains are still scanning five times a second; is this good or bad, safe or dangerous, harmful or helpful? These days, though, with fewer bears to fret about, our minds go to extraordinary lengths to spot dangers elsewhere. We can't help it![27]

What if I fail, embarrass myself, miss an open goal, say the wrong thing, arrive late, get picked on, look uncool . . .

Professor Paul McGee likens the human brain to an over-sensitive smoke alarm that is not only activated by a serious threat – the kitchen is on fire – but also by the equivalent of slightly overdone toast.

Remember, your mind thinks this is helpful. It's trying to do you a favour, to look after you, protect you from harm, save your skin. As a result we spend a lot of time gripped in a double whammy of worrying about things that, more often than not, (a) aren't worth worrying about and (b) will most probably not even happen.

Metaphorically, we're continually leaping around the kitchen wafting a tea towel at the smoke alarm, trying to quieten it down.

So if you're feeling anxious, congratulations! Your mind's doing exactly what it evolved to do.[28] Remember, this so-called negativity bias is fitted into every human.

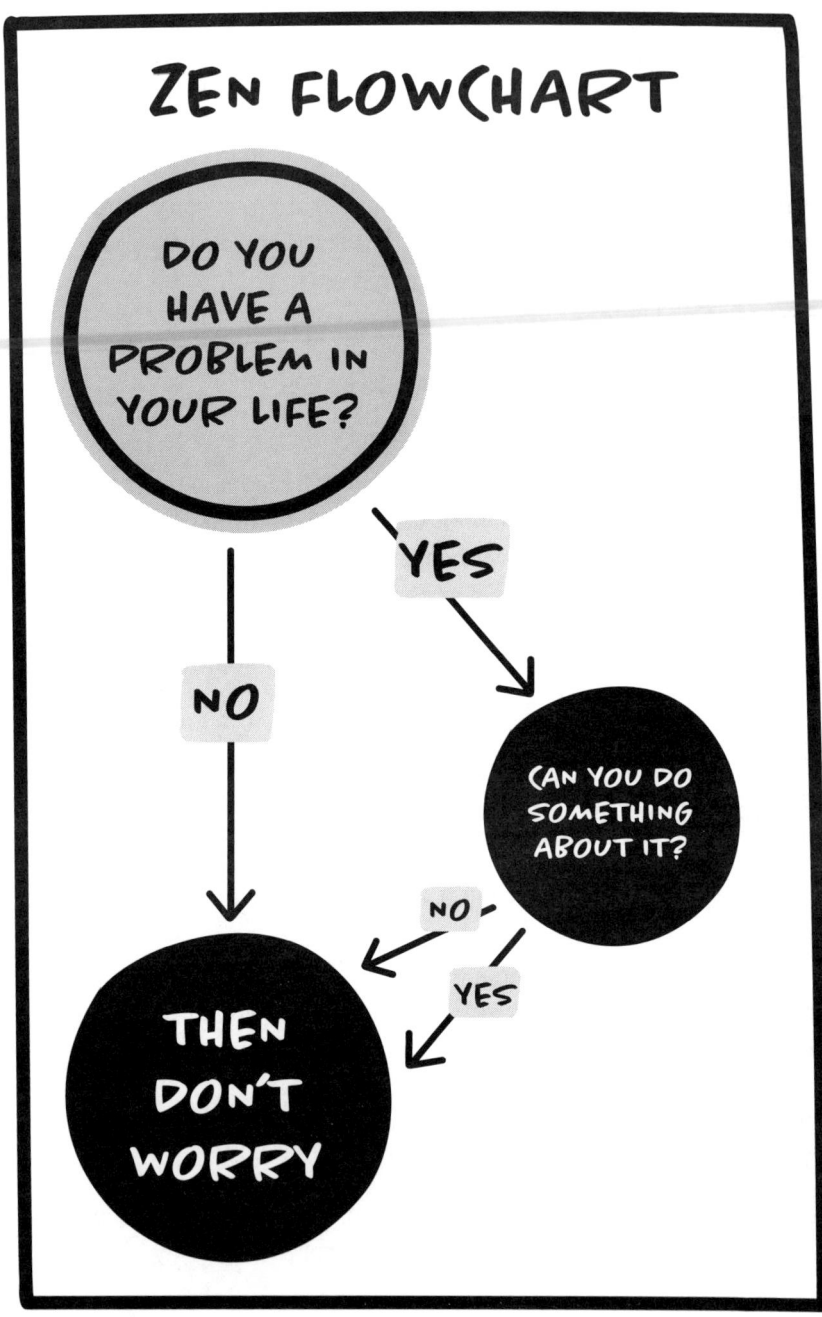

Hang in there, good news is coming, but first we have to layer on the truth. Back to our Richter scale analogy, while most of us are lucky to have avoided actual earthquakes, we've been experiencing 21st-century 'change-quakes' and their associated aftershocks.

If there's no prospect of the needle of change calming itself, there's really only one viable long-term strategy – to learn to be the kind of person who thrives in a fast-paced world. Someone who embraces change, who has an ability to bounce back and enough courage to stick a middle finger up to the world when it does its absolute worst.

Uncertainty isn't *in* your way. It is *the* way.

A 9.6 change-quake? *Bring. It. On!*

Zoochosis

Compare your lifestyle with that of someone from 100 years ago and at first glance it looks amazing. No, not perfect but amazing. For a start, if you look at the data, we're about nine times richer than back then, which means we can buy way more stuff. You've got technology, free education, a national health service, supermarkets full of food, central heating, electricity, electric cars, planes, indoor toilets, soft loo roll, movies/music streamed to your device, pizza . . . it's a world of abundance and yet we're more anxious, stressed and depressed than any other humans in the history of our planet.[29]

We have everything our ancestors could ever have dreamed of, and yet we're still not happy!

There are plenty of plausible explanations for the rise and rise of worry, anxiety and panic. Devil's advocate, just for a second, it could be that we've been birthing a batch of faulty human beings. Everyone's heard of the 'snowflake' generation but the only way to test it would be to transplant your average person from the 17th century, plonk them in today's hurly-burly world and track how they get on. Would they be tougher and more resilient? Would they cope just fine?

Would they heck! Give them 43 WhatsApp groups to respond to, introduce them to social media, teach them about selfies, get them to choose and pay for a coffee using their phone, scan a QR code, attend a virtual meeting and explain microwave meals to them. Day one, their heads would explode.

Which leaves us with the prospect that if humans haven't changed, there must be something in the environment that's causing us to go haywire.

Let's take that idea as our starting point.

Back when Ollie was a little kid, I took him and his sister to the zoo. We had a wonderful day watching the penguins guzzling their herring lunch, the elephants being cleaned with giant extendable brushes and orangutans doing their tyre-swinging party piece.

But, as an adult, I noticed something the kids missed. The animals were behaving strangely. The monkeys had scratched themselves 'till they bled. The proud silverback had embarrassing bald patches. The elephants were swaying, the lions were chewing the bars of their cage and the bears had worn a path with all their pacing up and down.

Note, this was not a bad zoo, nor is this an anti-zoo rant. But an Internet search took me to the word that describes this obsessive, repetitive behaviour: *zoochosis*.

Stated simply, captive animals become 'zoochotic'. They're suffering from extreme stress which seems strange because, in theory, the zoo environment has everything an animal could ever need: their meals come regularly without having to hunt, they don't have to worry about being attacked by predators, and they even get a full dental plan!

However, these creatures have won their physical safety at the expense of their psychological safety. These 'wild' animals are living lives of extreme sensory deprivation. Here they are, banged up 24/7, pacing, circling, rocking, scratching, swaying, over-grooming, bar-biting, self-harming – these behaviours result from frustration, stress and boredom.[30]

So what does a caring society do when animals develop zoochosis?

The answer – the zoo vets ease the animals' mental suffering with various forms of medication. Our point? They give them pills to ease their symptoms, when in actual fact it's a non-medical problem.

They're in captivity. *That's the problem*.

So, here's a series of interesting (and very big) thoughts, what-ifs and questions . . .

Have humans accidentally 'caged' themselves? Have we somehow built an environment that's not good for our health? Are *Homo sapiens* suffering from zoochosis? Are we metaphorically 'chewing the bars'? Big cities, fast food, sitting down, smartphones, next day delivery, screen time, working from home, binge watching . . . the modern world has bent over backwards to accommodate our every need. It's given us what we *thought* we needed. But have ease, convenience, comfort and safety come at a price?

Are we paying with our mental health?

Which leads to a real biggy of a thought: with about 20% of the population now diagnosed with some form of neurodivergency (dyslexia, dyspraxia, etc.)[31] and boys outnumbering girls by 4:1 on ADHD,[32] what if attention disorders are not an individual problem? What if *society's* got ADHD?

Let's look at one small example of how the world might be messing with our heads.

Since forever, humans haven't had screens and then, all of a sudden, about 20 years ago, everyone has screens, several in fact.

And guess what, anxiety has skyrocketed in the last 20 years.

Coincidence or human zoochosis?

Hey, I'm not a doom monger. Far from it. I love spending time online but it's all about balance. Yes, I want the ease of modern life that these amazing gadgets provide, but I also want to achieve some big goals, create strong relationships with those closest to me and, without wishing to sound too cheesy, I do actually want to live my best life.

I'm guessing you do too?

So watch out for human zoochosis. You'll see humans glued to screens, earphones in, eyes locked onto a device, a bit like zombies. It's not a great environment for humans.

It's no wonder that we're metaphorically 'chewing the bars'.

So, to combat zoochosis, set yourself free. Run, play, wander, have adventures, make mistakes, be silly, get lost in the woods, explore, build dens, travel, swim, laugh, strive, fail, sleep . . . but most of all, build strong relationships with your tribe . . . that's the perfect human environment.

In your opinion, how much screen time is ideal for perfect human wellbeing ? (asking for a friend)

Chapter 3

TEENAGE BOY
USER MANUAL

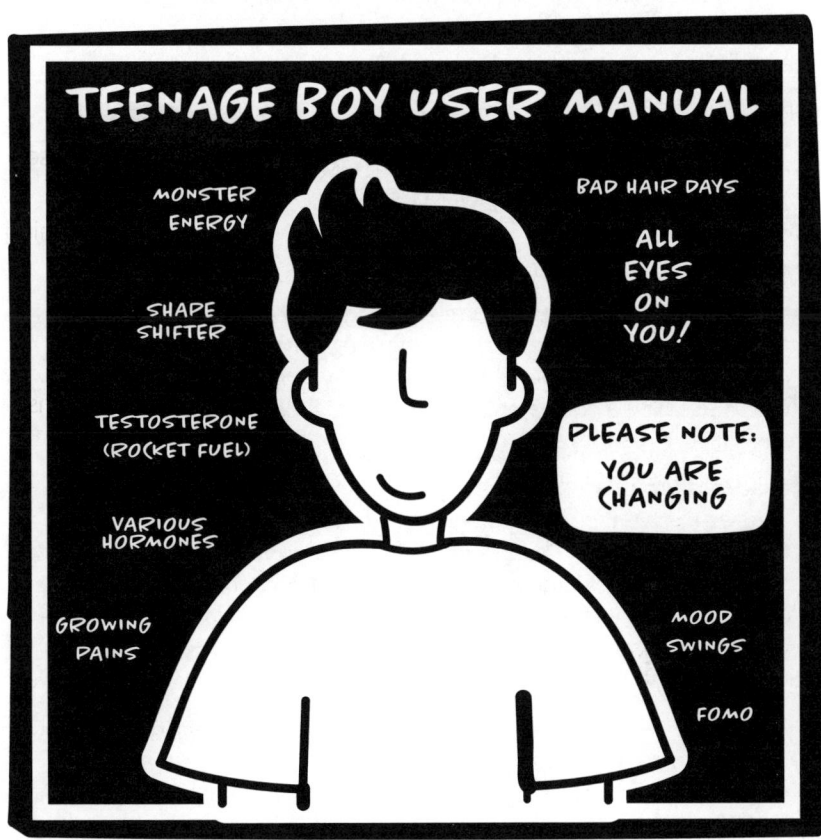

Chapter Summary

Boys will be boys, right? Well, yes, mostly. But not all boys are the same. This chapter gets to grips with phases of development and the various hormones buzzing around the teenage boy's body, focusing primarily on testosterone. What is it, why does it matter, and how can you make the most of this naturally occurring hormonal rocket fuel?

There's a rhyme that suggests boys are made of slugs and snails, whereas girls are sugar and spice and all things nice. Seems harsh on the male of the species, and if you are in fact made of slugs and snails, please seek urgent medical help. We'll tell you what you're truly made of as well as explain why you leave your homework until the last minute.

We keep it real by explaining a few male/female differences. Good news lads, we have bigger heads and bigger brains than girls and are way ahead in gaming but lagging in reading and writing. The overall conclusion is that to be the best young man you can be, it's worth stealing a couple of ideas from the girls.

There's a new acronym in town. We introduce FOPO and stick our shades on to stare into the glare of the Spotlight Effect. From then on it's a snooze fest where we remind you of the smallest thing that will make the biggest difference to your testosterone, energy, wellbeing, alertness and drop-dead-gorgeousness, which is, quite simply, sleep. There's a top tip on how to win the lottery and our finale is a letter from someone very (very) close to you.

There's a lot to get through. Let's crack on . . .

It's just a phase

It turns out that there are some basic phases of development that we *all* go through, and you're in the middle of one right now. We'll be super-brief, but if you understand the headline news, it might help explain a few things.

First up, there's plenty of human development while you're swimming around in your mum's tum. Your gender is determined at the moment of conception, when, in your case, the sperm contributed a Y chromosome, which created a boy. But all human foetuses start off as female until about seven or eight weeks later when testosterone kicks in and you transform into a boy.[33]

After about nine months you make a grand entrance into this world. Day one is normally a tough day on all concerned but things soon settle down and you soak up the world around you. You are a learning machine. Up until about eighteen months, babies have no sense of self. An infant can't look in the mirror and not recognise itself.[34] You were an experiencer, a blank slate; as an infant your brain was a buzzing hive of connectivity.

From two to ten you became what psychologists call 'adult-centred'. Mum, dad, gran, they are like gods. You hugged and worshipped them. Once you developed secure attachments with adults you had confidence to go explore your world.

Fast forward to right now. Your brain develops from back to front so you should have mastered all the back brain stuff like walking, talking, balancing, throwing and controlling your bowels (fingers crossed on that one) but the front bit is still under construction. There's a major teenage wiring job going on. Let me explain.

As you approach your teenage years your emotional system goes into overdrive. Cue a whole lot of classic teenage behaviours; social sensitivity, mood swings and self-doubt.[35] These 'growing pains' might challenge you, but they don't have to defeat you.

The teenage boy brain squirts dopamine in big quantities. We seek out pleasure, we experiment and take silly risks. (I say 'we' because it's not just you. Anyone who's reached the ripe old age of 16 has been through the same).[36]

The front part of the human brain, the bit that's still under construction, is the thinking brain. This develops *after* your emotional system, which means your brain doesn't really have a handbrake in the teenage years.

That's why teenagers stomp around not quite knowing what they're feeling, why they're feeling it or what to do about it!

The teenage brain isn't very good at planning. That's why you forget your PE kit, can't find your bus pass and leave your homework until the very last minute. Your under-developed prefrontal cortex also means that you lack the higher-order ability to act with consequences in mind. You follow the crowd (sometimes even when you know it's not a great idea), you question authority, kick back, push the boundaries and develop your own views and ideas about how the world works.[37]

You're not right, but you absolutely *think* you are.

You become what psychologists call 'peer-group centred'. Teenagers experience an overwhelming desire to fit in. This explains why you dress the same as your friends. I am guessing the same haircut and music too? Your tribe becomes all-important and your family can become very uncool. You'll be drawn to influencers and role models. All the Premiership footballers have tattoos, so you crave one too.

Developments between your ears are changing how you experience the world. Up until the age of about ten you didn't care what anyone thought about you. Think back to primary school, you'd stick your hand up to every single question and sing your loudest and proudest in school assembly. All of a sudden, you become a teenager and all that changes. You start having thoughts or opinions about other people and, BOOM, you realise other people are capable of having the same thoughts about you.

You become self-conscious and everything changes. Instead of being a happy-go-lucky kid without a care in the world, you start second-guessing what other people are thinking about you.[38] Self-doubt kicks in. Life becomes a 'fitting in' game. You become *hyper*-sensitive. You'll be blushing a lot. Don't take it personally; all primates go through these phases. There's not much you can do about the phases of human development, but we thought it might be useful to know what's going on so next time you get embarrassed, or you end up doing something stupid to fit in, you can blame evolution.

Main character syndrome

The good news is that most humans navigate the choppy teenage years perfectly well and things eventually settle down. Your brain is fully developed by your mid-20s and the vast majority emerge into the adult world just fine. As, we're sure, you will.

To help, here's something that's new, interesting and useful to know. Have you ever walked into a room and felt as though everyone was looking at you? Of course you have – *we all have* – it's called the spotlight effect. It describes the tendency to believe that others are paying more attention to us than they actually are – in other words, to always feel like we're 'in the spotlight'.[39]

Psychology, by nature, can be quite a serious subject but the experiment that discovered the spotlight effect is a rare gem. Students had to enter a room wearing the most uncool T-shirt imaginable (imagine the face of a pop star who was excruciatingly embarrassing) and researchers found that although they were expecting to be laughed at or ridiculed, in actual fact nobody noticed!

Translated to everyday life; everyone has 'bad hair days', or mornings where they've woken up to find an angry red pimple on their face, or got an answer totally wrong, or had to say a sentence out loud in French. You assume everyone is going to notice and probably laugh, or talk about you behind your back.

But the spotlight effect is a trick of the mind. Nobody really cares about your unruly hair, your pimple, your wrong answer or your terrible *'Je m'appelle'*. They're too busy standing in their own spotlight effect to worry about you. In fact, awareness of the spotlight effect and understanding that it's an illusion means you can relax and be yourself in social situations.

It's helpful to work the theory the other way. Ask yourself how you'd react if the roles were reversed. Take a moment to consider how you would feel if you were on the other side of the equation. In fact, on many occasions, you've probably been in class where your bestie has got bad hair and a pimple, and someone has stuck their hand up with the exact *wrong* answers and spoken French with a strong British accent. These episodes probably didn't register very highly on your radar. Yes, the person who did them felt mortified, but you hardly noticed.

The spotlight effect can hold you back. If it feels as though all eyes are on you, self-consciousness and anxiety kick in. The psychology gets complicated. Instead of relaxing into 'being you', you get anxious about how you think you're coming across to others. You try and look cool or perfect. It's hard work and stressful!

The reason we're telling you about the spotlight effect is because an over-inflated feeling of visibility is a phase that most teenagers go through. There's a time in your life – usually between about 12 and 16 – when you really do feel that all eyes are upon you.

The spotlight effect can feel very real and very dazzling. But it's neither. I don't want to burst your bubble but most people are too busy thinking about themselves to pay any attention to you!

Moving forward, here's something similar but subtly different.

FOMO, YOLO, LOL, FYI, IMO, BFF, TBH . . . the English language has thrown some interesting acronyms our way. Here's one to add to the collection – FOPO: *fear of people's opinions*.

The human brain is a magnificent piece of kit, but it's got some serious flaws. It's evolved over the last 200,000 years, but rather than start from scratch, evolution has added bits and patched over the glitches. One thing that hasn't changed is our craving for social approval. Back in olden times, you couldn't survive on your own. For your physical and emotional safety, you needed a team, tribe, clan or community. Boiling it down to its bare bones, a single human cannot bring down an antelope or capture a boar – *but a team can*. In fact, being excluded from your tribe was a death sentence, so fitting in was a matter of survival.[40]

Today, thanks to the explosion of social media and the intense pressure to fit in, fear of people's opinions is running rampant. We strive to see ourselves through the eyes of others.[41] You choose what trainers to wear, what bag to carry, what music to listen to, which team to support, what to post (etc.) partly while considering what other people will think. In fact, your whole identity is built on gaining approval from your 'tribe'.

Combined, FOPO and the spotlight effect can feel like full-beam headlights.

Simply recognising that most people, to varying degrees, are moving through the world under their own spotlight can help override your emotional programming. The moment you realise *we're all being dazzled by our own spotlight*, your relationship with FOPO will change.

The glare is not someone shining a spotlight on you. You are shining the spotlight on yourself, so maybe it's time to turn it down. We are wired to care about what others think of us. The key to valuing our opinions of ourselves over what others think of us is to know and accept ourselves. If you can genuinely know that you're a kind, warm-hearted, loving human being, then you can stop pretending and just crack on.

Here's the bare-knuckled truth. The kind, warm-hearted, loving version of you will still mess up. It doesn't mean that you won't occasionally say the wrong thing, make a lazy comment or misjudge a situation – but if you know in your heart of hearts that you're a good person, FOPO will be less exhausting and the spotlight effect less blinding.

Science says . . .

What's in a name?

Researchers discovered that professional baseball players with positive initials (examples: A.C.E., J.O.Y., W.O.W., N.E.W. and W.E.L.) live an average of thirteen years longer than players with negative initials (examples: B.U.M., P.I.G., D.U.D., S.I.N. and A.S.S.).

Thirteen years longer!

Another study found that successful people had names that were closer to the front end of the alphabet, so, for example, Aaron Adams is more likely to take the world by storm than Zane Zimmerman.

Thankfully, it's not an *exact* science.

It's a hormone thing

We're about to highlight some male/female differences that cause some people to get very hot under the collar. The reason we're including this information is because there's a lot of fake and misleading news out there and some very dubious advice.

Note, this hot-under-the-collar stuff is a fairly recent phenomenon. Two generations ago, people's collars were a lot cooler because the debate was way less fiery. It's another area where the heat has been stoked by social media. Do the stereotypical male/female differences hold up to scientific scrutiny? Are boys really more aggressive and girls really more empathetic, or do we just see what we expect in them? Where true sex differences do exist, are those disparities inborn or are they shaped by society? Why is it that men and boys are more prone to violence than women and girls? Why are 99% of gang members in London male?[42] What is it about young men that makes them *potentially* dangerous?

And, of course, the biggie, who's cleverer, boys or girls?

Disclaimer. Before we kick off, in the study of child development, no scientific discovery applies to 100% of people 100% of the time. There's no one size fits all. We'll be talking about scientific averages. The only rule is that there are exceptions to the rule!

One thing all humans have in common is that we consist of eight pints of blood and a whole load of self-created chemicals wrapped in skin.

HUMAN BEING INGREDIENTS:

CONTENTS MAY VARY IN COLOUR, SHAPE, AND BELIEFS

100% ORGANIC

GLUTEN FREE

100% AWESOMENESS, INTELLIGENCE, HUMOUR, A HINT OF MISCHIEF, A SMIDGE OF CHAOS AND DASH OF BAD DECISIONS.

NO ARTIFICIAL INTELLIGENCE ADDED.

SOME HUMANS ARE A LITTLE NUTTY.

FRAGILE   EMOTIONAL   MADE   HANDLE   REQUIRES
           BEING   WITH   WITH   COFFEE
                        LOVE   CARE

Men and women have more similarities than differences but one ingredient that differentiates males and females is hormones, particularly *testosterone*. Produced in the testicles (very important kit, please look after them), teenage/adult males generally have much higher testosterone levels than females. It starts in the womb[43] and may partly explain why boys are more fidgety and physically active than girls. Boys' and girls' motor skills develop differently,[44] possibly because of slight differences in brain development. This means boys kick, swing their arms and race around the house noticeably more than girls do[45], as many exhausted parents can testify.[46] That said, parenting might also be a factor. There's evidence to suggest that parents tend to discourage their daughters from physical risk, less so their sons.[47] Friendship groups push this even further. In an all-boy group, energetic lads feed off one another, climbing higher, riding faster, burping louder, being sillier and trying ridiculous new skateboard tricks.[48]

Controversial (but backed by research), given a choice of toys, preschool-age boys will tend to choose a truck and girls a doll.[49] Note, even male and female monkeys may show a modest preference for gender-stereotyped toys,[50] which suggests that there is something about vehicles, balls and moving parts that may resonate with boys' hormonal priming. By age five, girls show greater flexibility, choosing 'boy' toys and 'girl' toys equally. Boys, however, rarely do this crossover. Girls today are allowed – and hugely encouraged – to play sports, wear trousers and play with Lego much more than boys are encouraged to wear dresses and give the family dog a makeover.

Again, we're talking 'in general'. There are exceptions.

One of testosterone's main physical effects is that it causes muscle growth.[51] You might have heard about athletes getting banned for being caught taking 'steroids', which are basically just testosterone. Steroids allow athletes to build more muscle and recover faster, giving them an unfair advantage.[52]

There's plenty of evidence to suggest that steroids are *very* bad for your health. Yes, you might build some impressive biceps but you'll also be shrinking your testicles, losing your hair and shortening your lifespan.[53] Plus, if bulging biceps are your thing, with time and dedication it's perfectly possible to achieve that look naturally.

Body image – an important side note

Traditionally, body image and eating disorders have been much more common in young women and girls, but the past decade has seen an unprecedented rise in body image concerns amongst teenage boys and young men. Take a look at action movie superstars from the 2000s and compare them with the blockbusters of today, and you'll see characters getting bigger and more ripped as the years go by. Add on social media, where filtered, carefully selected images of men (who are often on steroids) are abundant, and it starts to make sense where the problem might be coming from.

Young men today are surrounded by unrealistic images of influencers with top 1% genetics who are on performance-enhancing drugs and are going to the gym in an effort to look ripped.

Going to the gym is not a bad thing; it's great to exercise and to get in shape. But doing it to try to achieve an unrealistic ideal is starting from the wrong place. Simply put, on social media there will *always* be someone who looks 'better' than you or lifts more than you, so setting *that* as your standard is setting yourself up to be miserable.

Trust me, I've been there.

If you want to exercise and change your physique, go for it. But start from a place of care; don't exercise because you hate the way you look. Find something you enjoy and exercise because it makes you feel good. What matters is that your body is healthy, not how huge or ripped you are. The discipline you'll learn from showing up and getting your body moving, however you do it, is far more valuable than how big your pecs are.

You're not a better man because you can bench press more than you could last year; you're a better man because you did something difficult, over and over again and didn't give up.

Testosterone also increases feelings of motivation and can make you feel more confident.[54,55] Scientists have even found that men who are given a tiny boost of extra testosterone are less likely to give up when they are facing a tough opponent.[56] But testosterone can also tip your fighting spirit over the edge into full-on aggression. It can make it harder for you to control your impulses, which means it's more difficult to stop yourself from doing things you shouldn't.[57] This could be one of the reasons why men convicted of violent crimes are often found to have higher testosterone levels than normal.[58]

Testosterone is really powerful stuff and not having enough of it is associated with a whole range of problems in men. Men who don't have enough testosterone tend to feel more depressed,[59] less motivated, more tired and experience weight gain.[60] Low testosterone is actually considered a medical issue, meaning people who don't have enough can get extra testosterone administered by a doctor. Our pets give us a great example of this, as male dogs and cats that have been neutered (meaning the lads' testicles have been removed . . . *ouch*) display much less aggressive or dominant behaviour compared to dogs that still have their bits intact.[61]

When you're younger and haven't hit puberty yet, your testosterone levels will be similar to the girls around you. However, at some point during your teenage years your testosterone levels will skyrocket, multiplying by around 30 times! This surge in testosterone is what's responsible for a lot of your teenage growth, your voice dropping, your facial/body hair beginning to grow as well as less pleasant things like body odour and acne.[62] Different boys get this surge at different times, so if it hasn't happened yet then don't stress and don't compare yourself to that one lad who's been able to grow full sideburns and a tash since he was 12. Every school year has one.

On the topic of comparing ourselves to each other, another interesting effect of testosterone is that it makes you want to engage in behaviours that make you feel in charge or 'dominant' in a social situation.[63] However, this works like a two-way street because when something happens that makes us feel dominant, that also causes our testosterone to increase.[64] This includes things like winning at a game (whether it is sports or video games),[65] when our favourite sports team wins a match[66,67] or when we feel like other people admire us.[68] So, winning gives us a testosterone boost, which then makes us want to succeed even more. Essentially, testosterone can make you want to seek out the competition, win the contest (game, fight, challenge, test) and be the top dog.

Girls score higher on many measures of empathy and are a bit more sensitive to other people's faces and emotions.[69] They carry this advantage into womanhood. Tuning into emotions, understanding how people feel . . . yes, boys can do it, but research shows that women have more of a natural in-built ability. This explains why your mum knows all your friends' names and your friends' mums, and your dad's not got a clue![70] It might also help to explain why females are less aggressive – it's hard to attack someone if you are acutely aware of what he or she is feeling.[71] That being said, girls can still get nasty but tend to use words rather than fists, which is called 'Indirect Aggression'.[72] Gossip, whispers, cruel text messages and social exclusion leave more scars in competitors' minds than on their bodies.

So, while testosterone does have its downsides, on the whole it is pretty good stuff. Not because it will make you an 'alpha male' or help you 'dominate' other people, but because it will make you confident (in fact, people who feel the need to dominate others all the time probably do so because inside they lack confidence), it will give you a sense of drive and it is important for your health.

With that in mind, it makes sense for us to do what we can to keep your testosterone levels where they need to be to reap all the benefits that our biology gives us. Remember, you will be coming up to your peak levels towards the end of your teens, so it makes sense to get as much as we can out of the human chemical gold rush.

Of course, everyone's testosterone levels will differ naturally; some people have a lot, some people have less, so it is not about having more than everyone else, it is about doing what is best for you.

Tips on how to increase your testosterone levels (known as test-maxxing)[73] are becoming more common around the internet. Social media and YouTube are awash with channels that claim to give you the *secret tips* on how to maximise your testosterone levels. This kind of content is becoming more popular with teenage boys,[74] but there is so much information that it can become confusing.

I just took a quick look on your behalf and quickly found a guide that listed a whopping 21 different supplements you should be taking in order to test-maxx, as well as explaining a huge laundry list of foods you should and should not avoid at all costs, with very dubious evidence. A lot of the advice on increasing testosterone levels comes from people trying to find something unique to say so that you will give them a click, a like or make a sale. You see someone on social media flaunting their amazing body and of course you want a body like that! *And they have the secret!* Hence you are lured in.

But here is the actual secret. You could take all of the supplements you can afford, eat a weird carnivore diet and take cold showers every day but none of these things will increase your testosterone as much as a few simple habits that come under the everyday banner of eat, move and sleep.

The irony is that a lot of teens and young men will spend money on supplements and do extreme things like ice baths to 'test-maxx', all while they drink energy drinks in the evening and stay up until 3 am playing video games. Time and time again research has proved that if you eat a healthy, balanced diet, exercise several times per week (it doesn't matter what exercise as long as it challenges you) and sleep eight to ten hours a night *consistently*, then your testosterone levels will be about as high as they can naturally be.[75] Could your levels be slightly higher with some raw eggs, yak's milk and supplements? Yes, *possibly*, but you should focus on getting the basic things right first before you consider any of the more out-there solutions.

Sleep, exercise and diet are all linked. Getting one of them right is good, but if the other two aren't right the benefits will be marginal. Most teens are chronically sleep deprived and under-exercised.[76,77] If you can get these two things right you'll already be miles ahead in the testosterone stakes. Just think about how much better you perform at basically anything when you've had a proper night's kip.

Some of you might already be getting enough exercise, in which case well done and keep going! Those of you who don't really exercise, we really do understand. There are so many things tempting you into bad habits. Our ancestors were constantly on the move, fighting for their survival, so our bodies have adapted to be active in order to be healthy. Getting into some sort of exercise routine might feel like hard work at the outset, but over time you'll feel far more energetic and confident.[78]

So do yourself a favour, make the most out of the body you were gifted. The more you look after it now, the better it will perform and the longer it will last. Imagine if in life you were only allowed to own one car, you were never allowed to buy a new one. You'd make damn sure you looked after that car, and you'd make sure to do everything you could to prevent problems from even happening in the first place. Your body is that car. You only get one, so look after it.

The next most obvious place to look for male/female differences is between your ears. Good news lads, we have larger brains (and heads) than females! Sadly, that doesn't show up in raw intelligence.[79] Girls have an advantage head start in words and then accelerate away from there. Girls begin talking about one month earlier than boys and are more than 10% ahead of boys in reading skills in pre-school.[80] Girls' advantage in reading and writing continues to grow through school, and females tend to outscore males on most measures of speaking, reading, writing and spelling throughout life. There is little proof that girls and women are better neurologically wired for reading, so the most likely explanation is quite simply the amount of reading children do for pleasure outside school. Put simply, girls read more than boys, and this additional exposure makes a difference in their academic performance that grows over time.

There's an obvious top tip right there for boys . . . well done on getting your head in this book, but don't stop here. Make *reading for pleasure* a habit.

READING CAN SERIOUSLY DAMAGE YOUR IGNORANCE

If girls have the advantage in language and reading, boys tend to have it in spatial awareness.[81] On average, we're better able to visualise and manipulate objects in time and three-dimensional space. The average man can perform mental rotation, that is, he can imagine how a complex object would look when turned around, better than up to 80% of women.[82] Spatial skills are important for success in several areas of science and higher maths, including calculus, trigonometry, physics and engineering.

Generally speaking, girls' brains reach maturity earlier than boys' do.[83] Brain differences are biological, but they are not necessarily fixed or hardwired. The crucial, often overlooked fact is that experience itself changes brain structure and function. Your brain has what neuroscientists call plasticity, meaning it's a shape-shifter. New neural pathways are being created and deleted all the time.[84]

As a teenager, you're slap bang in the middle of one of life's major developmental phases. You are changing. You are being shaped by natural internal forces and by the environment you find yourself in.

Appreciating how gender differences emerge gives you an insight into what's going on. But remember, humans are more alike than they are different. We're all flesh and blood creatures making it up as we go along. Take a lesson from the girls – pay attention to your fellow students, tune in to how they might be feeling. Remember, they're going through the same metamorphosis as you.

Sleep

A quick word about sleep. As a teenager, your body and brain are both shapeshifting from child to adult. Your body is working extra hard to regenerate, hence why you're tired. We're not wanting to nag but it's not very clever to deprive yourself of sleep, or to be up late playing games or texting, or waking up and checking your phone. To function properly you need between 8 and 10 hours' sleep a night.

Fact!

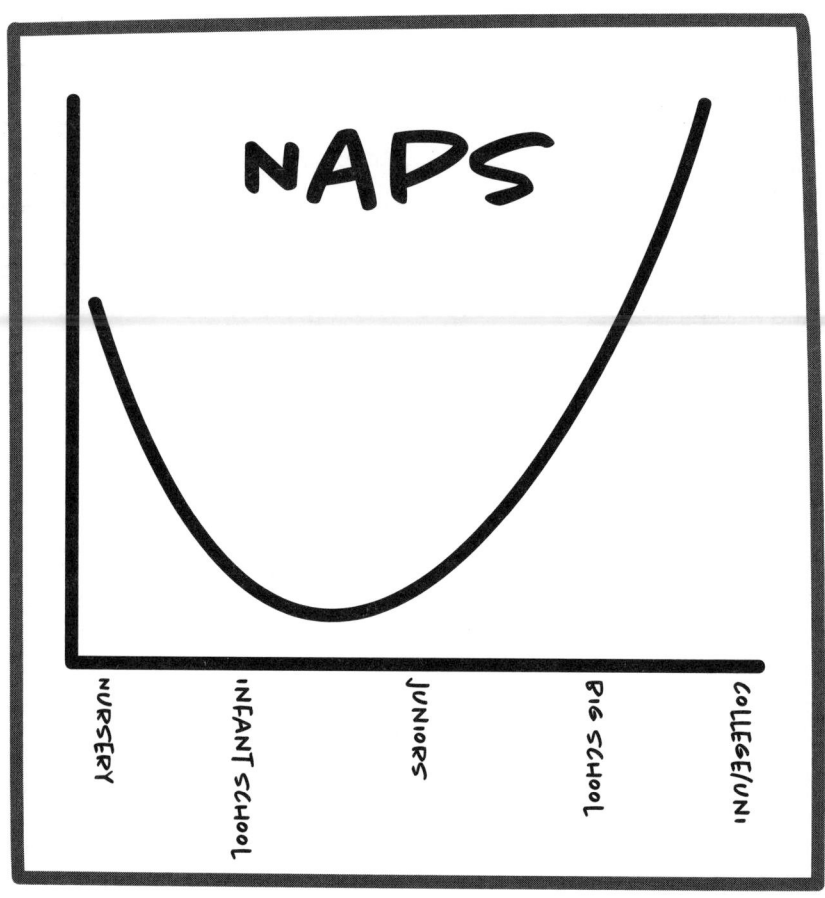

Let's keep it deadly simple. You've got to get up at 7am to be dressed, breakfasted and off to school. You can struggle out of bed, all groggy and grumbly about it being too early. You can slump to school tired and befuddled. Loads of teenagers do.

When we say loads of teenagers, we mean about 75% of them. Scientific research found that three out of every four teenagers are regularly not getting enough sleep during the school week and turning up to school tired.[76] This causes teenagers to develop something called 'sleep debt', where you get progressively more and more tired as the week goes on. Then, once the weekend rolls around, you oversleep to make up for the sleep debt you have accumulated throughout the week.

But what's wrong with a nice big lie-in at the weekend? Well, it turns out that oversleeping doesn't completely fix sleep debt, and that sleeping for more than 10 hours actually might make you even more tired than you would be if you slept a regular amount. This feeds into the vicious cycle of making you feel constantly tired even on weekends when you should be doing the things you love to do!

Now, in your defence, scientists have found that the circadian rhythms of teenagers are a bit delayed. Circadian rhythm is the fancy scientific term for body clock, so put simply: teenagers' body clocks are pushed back by a few hours, making them want to go to bed later and sleep in longer.[85]

So, it is more difficult for teenagers to get up in the morning than for adults, proven by science. But unfortunately, there is not a whole lot we can do about this. We can't expect entire societies to push everything back by a few hours just for you to have your scientifically verified lie-in. So, in short, yes it's tough, but you have to suck it up.

The secret is, of course, to go to bed a bit earlier. I mean, come on, it's the simplest solution in the entire book. A bedroom is called a BEDroom for a reason. Take responsibility for making it a screen-free zone. Remember, your brain and body are developing like crazy. You're asking a lot of them. Give them a break! Night time is an opportunity for them to go to work, re-wiring, upgrading and rebooting. Give your brain and body a fair chance by getting into good sleep habits.

If the reasoning above doesn't cut the mustard, then this should tip the balance in favour of getting to bed earlier and with no distractions. A British uni did a sleep study and calculated that getting into good sleep habits is equivalent to winning £120,000 a year on the lottery. Every year![86]

If you're still not convinced, here's a plea – in fact it's almost emotional blackmail – from someone who loves you dearly.

A brainy SOS

Hi. It's your brain here. You've been ignoring my recent warnings so I'm going old school and writing you a letter instead. It might seem a little weird, but please go with it. What follows is a heartfelt message from me (your brain) to you (your body) because life's phenomenal when we work together.

DEAR BODY.

I've been trying to grab your attention by making you lethargic and irritable. You know when you slump out of bed in a grump, that's me, sending you a warning. This is a heartfelt SOS from your grey matter; *help, I am struggling!*

And if I'm struggling, you will be too! Because you and I (brain and body), for richer or poorer, better or worse, till death us do part . . . we're lifelong partners. We need to work as a team.

Maybe you don't remember, but we've both always needed sleep. You used to sleep for 16 hours a day when you were a baby! Then, in primary school your bedtime was 7 pm. As we've gotten older you've started sleep cheating. It all kicked off when you got all those screens; 7 pm crept to 8, then 9. Then the smartphone appeared and your sleep patterns went haywire.

Here's something you probably don't know. When you're in the land of nod I take the opportunity to do some cleaning. During what's called your slow-wave sleep I open the brain/spinal fluid sluice gates and clear the waste.

It's true, I promise. Every single night, when you close your eyes, I rinse myself in a watery cerebrospinal fluid that flushes out toxic proteins and carries them to your liver where they're disposed of. Think of it like brain poop. It sounds a bit gross but when you're sleep deprived, you feel groggy and confused. It's because you've got a head full of ~~sh~~ brain poop. You're clogged up with cranial constipation.

Good quality sleep is brainwashing, but in a good way! I can only clean your brain poop while you're asleep. In awake mode, I'm crazy busy running your life; walking, talking, learning, thinking, feeling, calculating, reacting, anticipating – I've not got time to flush the brain poop.

Think of it like a house party. You can be in full-on party mode or you can clean up. It's hard to do both at the same time. So you party hard during the day, and then I clean up afterwards! That's how it works. Or at least, how it's *supposed* to work!

If you gave me more time, I could do a proper scrub and polish and you wouldn't be falling asleep in those morning lessons or be so damn grumpy with your parents.

Hey, I don't want to scare you, but over time that brain poop can build up and stink the whole place out. If you're sleep cheating, it makes it harder for me to help you do super important stuff like fighting cancer and other illnesses. Sleep should be an absolute #1 priority. It's clean and repair time.

So, a small request from me – can you remove all screens from the bedroom and leave your phone plugged in downstairs during the night? You might think listening to something helps you sleep, but in reality all that background noise does is distract me from doing my job of cleaning things up.

Look, I'm your brain. I need you to help transport me around and you need me to help you be smart. It's a win-win deal. If you commit to getting a quality night's sleep every night (not just on the weekends), then I'll help you have an amazing life.

Here's the clincher – have you ever wondered why it's sometimes called 'beauty sleep'? Because sleep makes you happier, less anxious, smarter and even more attractive – *seriously!*

I love you and getting our sleep right is the best way to love me and yourself back.

Yours cerebrally.

Your brain

Chapter 4

LIFE MAXXING

WHITE CHOCOLATE MOCHA FRAPPUCCINO, DECAF, DOUBLE BLENDED, ALMOND MILK, PUMPKIN FOAM, WITH CARAMEL DRIZZLE AND VEGAN WHIPPED TOPPING ANYONE?

Chapter Summary

Choice is good, right? Possibly, but not if you're experiencing 'choice overload'.

We invite you to create two possible futures, one easy and one much harder, with the advice to go hard. To help you wrestle back some control of your life, we introduce our Life Maxxing Matrix, steering you away from Time Bandits and towards the Game Changer zone.

We finish with the truth about school and why your most boring teacher might actually be setting you up for life.

But first, who's up for a white chocolate mocha frappuccino, decaf, double blended, almond milk, pumpkin foam with caramel drizzle and vegan whipped topping?

The paradox of choice

The unique father and son writing team gives us an opportunity to reflect on the generation gap. We both grew up in the same small market town in Middle England. Here is a grid that shows some changes that have happened in a single generation – see if you can spot the pattern. . .

	ANDY (DAD)	OLLIE (SON)
NUMBER OF SCREENS IN HOUSE	1 TV	3 TVS, 4 PHONES, 1 IPAD
NUMBER OF SCREENS AT LOCAL CINEMA	1 CINEMA, 1 SCREEN	3 MULTIPLEXES, 23 SCREENS IN TOTAL
NUMBER OF FREE TV CHANNELS	3	284
NUMBER OF POTENTIAL SUBSCRIPTION CHANNELS	0	112
TAKE-AWAYS ON LOCAL HIGH STREET	2 (BOTH CHIPPIES)	9 (INDIAN × 2, CHINESE × 2, ITALIAN × 3, THAI, CHIPPIE)
NUMBER OF COFFEE SHOPS	1 (GREASY SPOON CAFÉ)	7
TYPES OF COFFEE IN COFFEE SHOPS	1 (THE LITTLE DRINKING HOLE HADN'T BEEN INVENTED. NOBODY DRANK COFFEE ON THE GO)	37 (PLUS 3 SIZES, DRINK-IN OR TAKE-OUT, 7 TYPES OF MILK, 6 CHOICES OF FOAM AND 13 SYRUPS)

The pattern?

An explosion of choice. And choice is good, *right*?

Well, yes, *probably*? Up to a point. It is absolutely true that today's world is 'superior' if we measured it by how much choice we have. But, as with everything, you can have too much of a good thing.

Have you ever had one of those moments where you sit scrolling through YouTube and you just can't find a video worth watching, so you click around, hopping from clip to clip? Or where you keep opening different websites, apps or games but can't settle because none of them is hitting the mark?

If any of these situations sound familiar, then you've experienced the feeling of 'choice overload'.

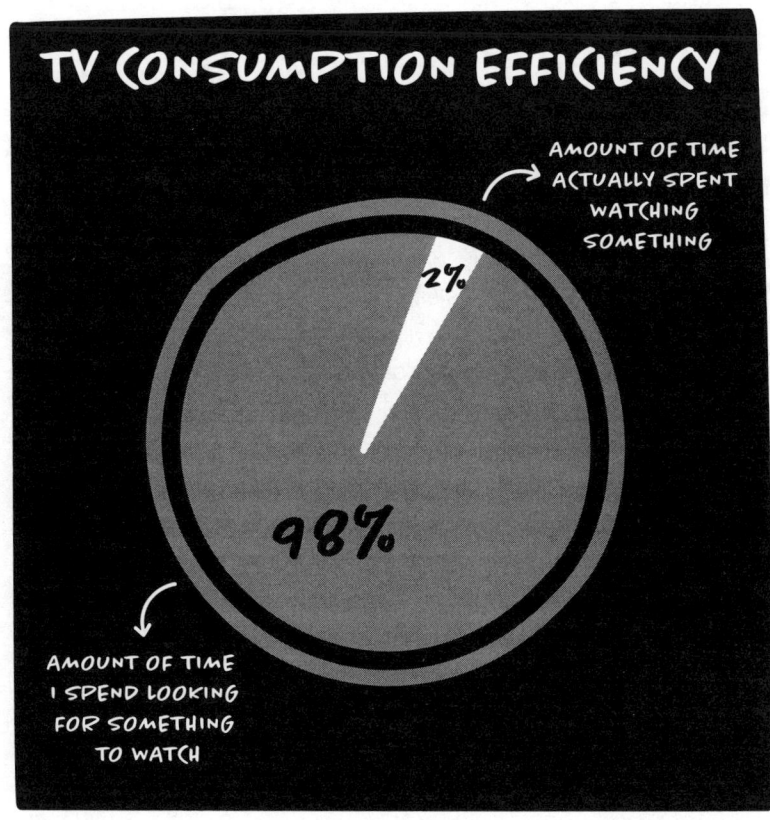

Psychologists and economists have found that too much choice actually makes us less happy. Choice overload (or 'overchoice') is a subset of FOMO. When you have dozens of alternatives, you are always going to feel like there *could* be a better option than what you end up choosing, even if that isn't true. So ironically, lots of choices make it harder for us to make a choice, and so we end up choosing nothing and just flipping in between.[87]

Not only is this a massive time waster, overchoice also makes it harder for us to do things that we *have* to do but might not necessarily *want* to, like homework or chores. With a thousand entertaining things at our fingertips, it's easy to get sucked into time wasting.

> I used to be a crastinator, but then I went pro.

It gets worse when we factor in the fact that our brains are inherently lazy. They like to save energy in case of an emergency, so day to day, minute by minute, they loop through a pattern of routines. This autopilot mode means that if you give yourself the option of doing something difficult versus something that's easy, you're naturally going to try and take the easy option. Your brain will do its best to convince you that a few more hours on a games console is a good choice or that you can leave your homework until the night before it's due. Your brain is *amazing* at finding excuses *not* to do things that it doesn't want to do.[88]

But here's the thing. If you look at anyone who's achieved something incredible – musicians, actors, singers, dancers, comedians, business-people, anyone who is super-successful – that person will have done a *lot* of things they don't want to do. There will have been hundreds of occasions where that person would have much preferred to watch TV or play video games, but they chose to ignore their brain's excuses and opt for activities that were less fun but *more* important.

It just so happens that you're inhabiting a world of abundant choice. Reflecting on the dad/son comparison grid from a few pages ago, to me, my dad's world looks horrific. *One* cinema with *one* screen! *One* café with *one* coffee. Growing up, he must have been gagging for a white chocolate mocha frappuccino, decaf, double blended, almond milk, pumpkin foam, with caramel drizzle and vegan whipped topping. In Venti size, to-go, with his name inked on the cup.

But of course, he wasn't craving any of that because it didn't exist. The marketing gurus hadn't thought it up. His generation was pre-change-quake. One coffee shop, one type of coffee, with a dash of full fat cow's milk, drink-in, no choice, no messing. Choice *under*-load! The world was a lot simpler and guess what, they didn't have the same mental health problems that we do today.

Hey, we're not blaming coffee shops for the mental health crisis, just calling it out as a simple everyday example of an explosion of choice in wider society.

> **Hit refresh**
>
> Quit being a control freak
>
> Resign from being the general manager of the entire world. You can't control everything and everyone. You're not responsible for anyone else's happiness. Stop trying to change the world, and start changing YOUR world.

The change agent

Cast your mind back to when you were five years old and just starting school. Up to that point you didn't really get much of a say in anything. Five years earlier, you'd arrived in the world and all your choices were made for you. You didn't choose your parents or where you were born. You didn't choose your name, your clothes, your meals, or your school.

Gradually, over time, you begin to grab the reins of your own life. As a teenager, you get to choose your clothes, your friends, your food, what to play, watch and listen to. Psychologists call it 'agency'. It means you have control. The crucial thing is to realise that the choices you make NOW, *will* affect your future.

With that in mind, here's a thought experiment. Imagine that you have travelled 20 years into the future but in *two different timelines*.

Future 1

In the first timeline you've been the bang average version of you. You spent 20 years chasing instant pleasure, so you've racked up thousands of hours of game time, your thumbs are champion scrollers and your back catalogue of porn is eye-watering. This easy distractibility means you lost your focus on schoolwork and became one of those last minute 'it'll do' homework merchants. School, *what's the point?* Twenty years later you're undercooked, underprepared, underperforming and have underachieved. Your lacklustre habits didn't seem to matter 20 years ago, but the chickens have come home to roost.

Picture your life. After two decades of mediocrity, what job are you doing? How might people describe you? How does this future feel?

Future 2

Imagine another timeline, one where you've spent the last 20 years going the extra mile. You spent 20 years making sure your important stuff was out of the way before starting your screen time, you threw yourself into every subject even if it wasn't your favourite (and you carried that mentality into adulthood), and you spent more of your free time on crafting skills that didn't involve screens. While others were distracted, you prepared, performed and achieved, and you still had plenty of time for fun. Same questions as in future one: after two decades of focus, what job are you doing? How might people describe you? How does *this* future feel?

You don't need to be a genius to realise that option two will likely turn out better. Everyone knows that the harder you work when you're younger, the better odds you have further down the line. But the modern world has organised itself to distract you.

You have a choice now about which of your two futures you want to aim for. The 'problem' with those two futures is that future one, the bang average one, is really easy to achieve.

Laziness pays off now whereas hard work pays off in the future. And we like 'easy' and 'immediate'. Of course we can't predict the future, but we can orient ourselves towards a particular path. The hand you were dealt at five years old wasn't your choice, but the hand that you play now absolutely is.

If it was easy to get on the right path, everyone would be doing it. But look around, the shortcuts are busy, and there are hardly any people on the extra mile.

We know that it's easy to procrastinate in a world that is *full* of interesting distractions.

Once you realise that the person with all the power to change it is the person staring back at you while you brush your teeth, things start to shift. That person has 'agency' (remember, that's a posh term that describes the ability to influence the direction of your life), which means you are the agent. The *change* agent.

With that in mind, here's something that will help . . .

Life Maxx-Matrix

You have certain responsibilities; things you *have* to do, but you also have a massive list of distractions; things that you'd much *prefer* to do! Chances are, the things on your distraction list are much more interesting.

It's safe to say that today's environment has been cunningly designed to grab your attention. It's so seductive that you can find yourself lost in a rabbit warren of disturbance. It's easy to be distracted from the distraction that distracted you from your original distraction!

Before you know it, it's Monday morning and, guess what, your homework hasn't magically written itself and your French vocab hasn't memorised itself. Cue a whole lot of self-imposed anxiety.

This interference problem is here to stay. The world is what it is. AI, algorithms, apps, social media – they're not suddenly going to pack their bags and disappear. They're just going to find even more sneaky ways to hijack your attention.

This gives rise to some very important questions:

1. How the heck can you stay focused in an ADHD environment?
2. How can you supercharge your productivity?
3. And when the list of tasks starts to stack up, *where the heck should you begin?*

Enter, centre stage, our fabulous Life-Maxxing Matrix. It'll help you wrestle back some control of your life.

The Life-Maxxing Matrix has two axes, one for effort (how easy is it for you) and the other for importance (how big an impact will it have on your life).

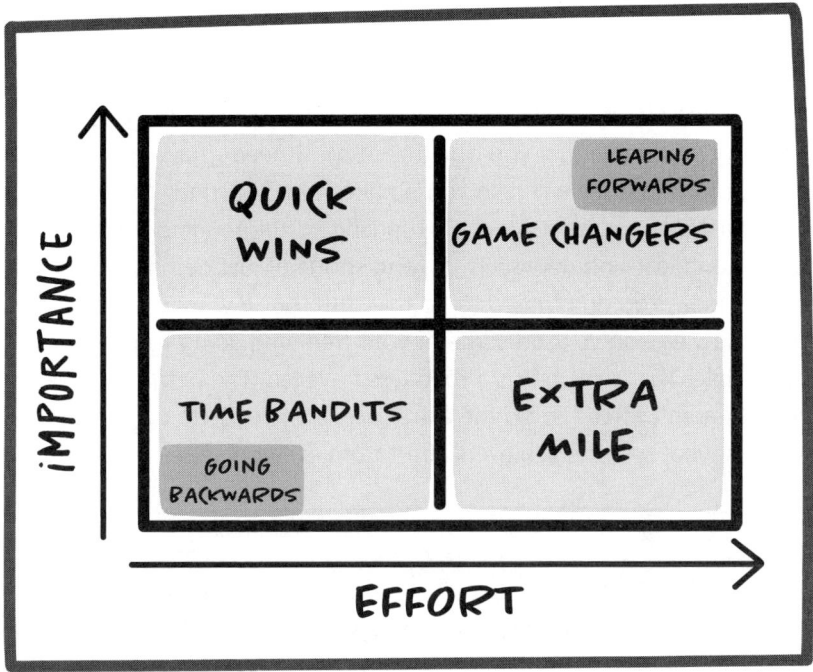

Let's give you a whistle-stop tour, starting bottom left in the all-too-familiar TIME BANDITS zone. These are tasks that are low in effort and importance. For example, playing another game on your console or scrolling on your phone. These activities are like junk food – hard to resist, easy to binge on, but they offer very little nutritional value to your life.

Beware, the TIME BANDITS are always lurking, waiting for an opportunity to steal your precious attention.

Top left are your QUICK WIN tasks that are important but that you find easy. For example, all homework is important but if art is your favourite subject it will feel like a low-effort task. Whisper these next few words quietly, *you might even enjoy it!*

Get stuck into these QUICK WINS and you'll gain some momentum. Once you're motoring, it's important that you stay in the groove so stay alert for the TIME BANDITS. There's always a first-person shooter game waiting to snaffle your attention.

Bottom right activities will stretch you. We call it the EXTRA MILE zone because it's for tasks that you don't necessarily *need* to do, but if you put the effort in, they will help you go above and beyond. This is stuff like extra work in subjects you're struggling with, spending time on hobbies and learning new skills, playing sports or just getting stuck into a good book. You don't *need* to do this stuff, but *if* you do it, you'll feel great knowing you've used some of your free time doing something worthwhile. The extra mile is a road less travelled. The people who lead the pack aren't forced to go the extra mile, they chose to do it, and that choice is what sets the achievers apart from everyone else.

'A habit missed once is a mistake. A habit missed twice is the start of a new habit.'
James Clear (best selling author)

Top right is GAME CHANGING stuff. These activities are important *and* they require effort. For example, revising for a big exam, whether you like the subject or not, is definitely high in importance *and* high in effort. Ditto completing a big piece of coursework. It's not all about school though; this zone can include things like learning to play the guitar or learning your lines for a school play. With GAME CHANGER activities, even if you're putting in max effort, they need lots of time dedicated to them to get the best results.

The problem with this zone is that it's easy to get distracted by simpler tasks in the other zones. That's why GAME CHANGER activities need scheduling. To nourish your future, you need to block off big chunks of distraction-free time to devote to GAME CHANGING activities.

Looping back to the TIME BANDIT zone, we're not killjoys. Things like screen time and just messing around with your mates and siblings – we aren't saying don't do these things, everyone needs to chill out occasionally. Our message is that you should save these things for when you've done the other stuff on your list. If you jump straight into chillout mode when you *know* that you have other stuff you need to do, that stuff will linger in the back of your mind, and you won't be able to enjoy your down time fully. So, the paradox is that by chilling out too much, you actually don't even end up chilling out at all!

Getting the other stuff on your Life-Maxxing Matrix done first means that, when the time to chill comes, you can *really* chill. Nothing is more relaxing than doing something you enjoy *when you know you've earned it!*

You'll have noticed that we've added two extra zones in the bottom left and top right. If you're *continually* pick-pocketed by the TIME BANDITS you will be GOING BACKWARDS. You will literally be losing ground to those who are focused elsewhere. Your skills, knowledge and attitude will be diminishing.

Note, if you recognise that you're currently in the habit of too much screen time, scrolling or vegging, it's not too late. This is your wake-up call. The Life Maxxing Matrix is designed to snap you into fresh new habits that will accelerate your potential.

Speaking of which, if you're wanting to take the world by storm, there really is no other way than doing the hard yards *consistently*. Hence the LEAPING FORWARDS box in the top right corner. Focusing on the GAME CHANGER tasks (BIG effort and BIG importance) *for a prolonged period of time* will reap huge rewards. You will experience giant leaps of learning and, although there are no guarantees, you will be improving the odds of having a stellar life. That second future that you thought about earlier – that incredibly bright one – it lives right here!

The general rule of thumb is that to become amazing at anything you need to devote ten thousand hours of genuine hard work and practice.

Ten thousand hours in the game-changer zone – is that easy? *Nope*. Is it worth it in the long run? *ABSOLUTELY*! Ten thousand hours might not be what you want to hear but it's basically the cheat code.

Our advice is to sketch out a Life-Maxxing Matrix and write down all the stuff you need to do this week, sorting it into the boxes. The crucial thing is to know what your Time Bandits and Game Changers are. Avoid the former, invest in the latter and it'll supercharge your productivity, allowing you to live a less stressed existence.

You'll be amazed what you can do with a clear head and all that extra time!

And finally, the truth about school is that we all have favourite subjects where everything clicks, and we all have the, *ahem*, total opposite.

Lots of teenagers will complain about the boring subjects because a lot of it seems pointless. I don't remember a single essay that I wrote in English, I've forgotten how to calculate all of the angles of a triangle, and my knowledge of kings and queens is long forgotten. If you're not the sporty type it's actually less painful to 'forget' your PE kit than to suffer a game of rugby.

It's only now, with the wonder of hindsight, that it all becomes clear. Just because you might not use some of the stuff you learn in school, doesn't mean there's no value. This is because the value doesn't necessarily come from the things you learn, but from the *process* of learning about them. Learning to learn is one of the best skills you can pick up, and learning to learn about stuff that maybe doesn't interest you is a *vital* skill. In fact, I'd go further by suggesting that sitting through totally boring lessons, but soaking up the learning, is one of the most important skills you'll ever pick up.

Trust me, English isn't really about English. Sure, on the face of it, while you're sat there it seems to be about Shakespeare, war poems or essays. But the real value comes from learning to dissect the real meaning, analyse the words and get your thoughts down on paper.

Maths isn't really about numbers. For sure, numbers will feature, but sitting through an hour of triangles and not being distracted by the idiots around you is a valuable skill to learn.

History is about the past, but it's also about right now. An hour of history is about learning to rock up on time, with a great attitude, game-face on, and a genuine interest in learning why things happened. That's such a valuable skill.

PE isn't really about sport. Sure, it helps if you're good enough to be able to hit a tennis ball, but the lessons are really about learning to work as a team, to communicate, to win with grace and/or lose with dignity.

Heads up, when you eventually get a job, there will be exciting bits but also hundreds of pointless, boring meetings. Rather than switching off or sticking your hand up and saying, 'Boss, I don't get it', you'll be expected to look interested, take notes, contribute some ideas, and learn something. Taking this to the extreme, next time you're sitting through the most tedious hour of Shakespeare with Mr Boring from Dullsville, you can stay behind and personally thank him. 'Sir, I see what you did there. That was mightily dull. Seriously Mr B, the ability to extract all the interest from a subject to leave it bland and flat is quite a talent. Big ups. Not everyone can do that. Thanks for preparing me for the world of work! You're a legend.'

You get the idea. Honestly, we're telling you now because you don't realise at the time.

Basically, even if the subject is bone dry, there's always a juicy learning opportunity. Be a learner, soak it up.

Chapter 5

TERMINALLY ONLINE

'I WISH I'D SPENT MORE TIME ON MY PHONE'

NOBODY'S SAID ON THEIR DEATHBED, EVER.

Chapter Summary

You might officially be Gen Alpha . . . but you're really Gen-Scroller, the very first generation that's grown up with unlimited internet access, social media, games consoles and artificial intelligence.

That's amazingly good news. *Unless* . . .

Binge screening is making you sick and damaging your future.

Standing back, objectively, and looking at our modern lives, we are where we are. Your parents' generation innocently welcomed smartphones into our lives. We rubbed the magic lamp, the Smartphone Genie was awakened, and it ain't going back in.

Genies don't rock up very often so we didn't want to waste the opportunity. You weren't around so we asked for three wishes on your behalf. They're probably the exact same three wishes that your parents want for you, and that, when the time comes, you'll want for your kids. The first two are obvious, but the third wish is the most important because it helps you achieve wishes one and two:

1. Happiness
2. Good health
3. That you learn to take charge of your phone rather than your phone taking charge of you.

The rest of this section is written to help you achieve wish three, which, by spooky coincidence, will help with wishes one and two.

Digi-decline

It started so innocently. TVs, laptops, smartphones, games consoles – they were all designed for light entertainment. To add value to your life.

Then social media came along and made it even more of a thrill. All of a sudden you could follow, share your thoughts and feelings, upload selfies, videos and keep in contact with friends, relatives *and celebs*! Then AI, which can be your coach and your 'friend'. It was all good, wholesome, innocent fun until, all of a sudden, *it wasn't*.

The latest survey suggests teenagers are spending nine hours a day in front of a screen,[89] of which 5+ hours of that is social media.[90] There's a feeling that we might have reached a tipping point where social has become anti-social and gaming (particularly in boys) has reached addictive levels.

Everything is okay in moderation, but you can become *terminally online*.

Check the list below. How many can you tick *honestly*?

I do solemnly swear that I . . .

- Prioritise human relationships *over followers*
- *Don't* reach for my phone every time I get a spare 10 seconds
- Am *not* glued to my games console
- Rarely, if ever, doom-scroll
- *Never* pester my mum/dad/stepdad/stepmum for a new, upgraded, faster, sleeker, better phone, latest game or more screentime
- *Never* bring my phone to the dinner table
- Don't know the family wi-fi password off by heart
- Am *not* causing my mum/dad/stepdad/stepmum to nag me to get off my phone and/or games console
- Live in a screen-free bedroom
- Am *not* signed up with any social media apps
- Am *not* following a whole range of celebs
- Am *not* at least a bit jealous of everyone else's lives
- *Haven't* practised taking hundreds of selfies in search for the perfect one
- Have *never* edited a photo to enhance my appearance
- Don't understand what this list is about because I *do not* own a smartphone or games console and am perfectly happy with the situation

That last one is crazy, right? There's only 1% of teenagers who reach age 14 without owning a smartphone.[89,91]

We're not expecting you to throw your smartphone into a lake and live off-grid, in a log cabin, wearing animal furs and extracting your own teeth. But whatever your starting point, we'd like to nudge you towards living a bit more 'phone lite'.

Why? Because if you're terminally online, valuable chunks of your life are ticking away. Most teenagers struggle to visualise the future so take it from someone who's 40 years ahead of you. 'I wish I'd spent more time on my phone,' is a sentence that nobody's said on their deathbed, *ever*.

Factor in the various mental health issues associated with excessive screen time, and without wanting to sound too heavy, **when the fun stops, STOP.**

We didn't boldly step forward and sign up for the digital world we find ourselves in. You, the teenager, didn't vote for it. You were born into it. Chances are you love it, because you don't know anything different!

The smartphone was sold on the promise of freedom and yet here we are, imprisoned!

The Japanese have a wonderful phrase, *hara hachi bu*, which means you should stop eating just before you're full.[92] It saves you from pigging out. We wonder if there's a digital equivalent? A bit of screen time is perfectly fine, but don't get bloated.

We've invented a new illness for modern times and we're calling it the 'Digi-Decline'. Beware, it's a slippery slope!

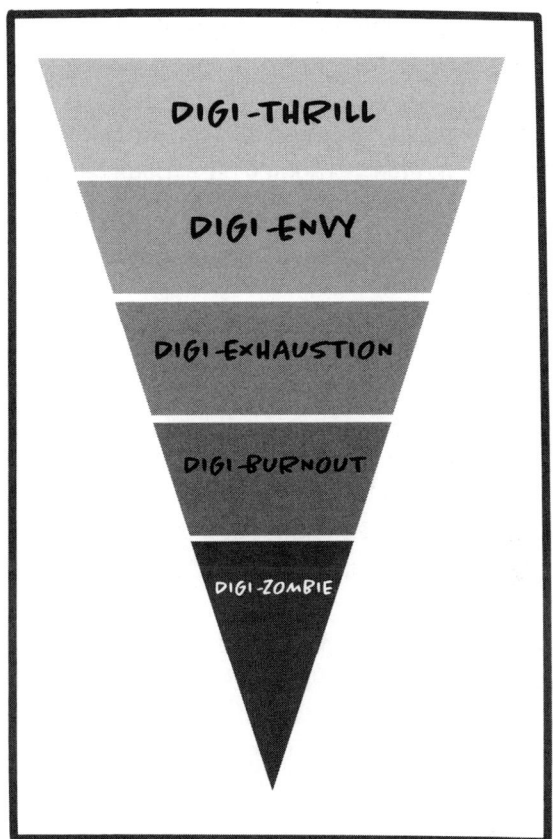

Starting innocently, the DIGI-THRILL phase comes with your first phone. To be fair, it might be your dad's old one but it's passed down to you. Your actual own phone. The thrill of it!

You might strike the jackpot with a top-of-the-range all-singing-all-dancing super-sleek rectangle that makes your mates drool, but far more likely your first phone is actually a bit rubbish. It might even be one of those that can't get onto the internet, in which case you'll soon be experiencing DIGI-ENVY.

This causes you to nag and nag until your parents give in and you're upgraded to something more in keeping with the modern teenager. The world of apps opens up and, of course, each app is perfectly fine in isolation. You download it because it has merit, but the combined noise of so many shiny, attention-grabbing, mood-manipulating apps is deafening.

The urge to check your feed or to mindlessly scroll, looking for a pellet of something nourishing – *anything* – is a form of addiction.[93] You start to feel uncomfortable. DIGI-EXHAUSTION has kicked in. You're losing control of time. You're an intelligent human being with a life to live and you know screens are a bad use of your time, but here you are anyway.

DIGI-BURNOUT occurs after prolonged digi-exhaustion. We're defining it as mental and emotional depletion that's experienced after prolonged periods of digital exhaustion. It's not so much of a thrill anymore, more of an obsession. You're absent, even when in the same room. Checking your 'likes' is strangely addictive. The black rectangle is a digital slot machine. You're not weak willed or stupid. So why can't you stop looking?

The innocent days of digi-thrill are long gone. Although you entered cyberspace innocently, bright eyed and curious, what you didn't realise is that the doors got locked. You're trapped. There are thousands of Silicon Valley geeks and billions of dollars invested in keeping you there!

These levels have sucked you in, but you can still claw your way out. If you don't, there's a darker level, the DIGI-ZOMBIES who live with their curtains drawn. Neither dead nor alive, they're in the grips of a near-life experience.

DIGI-ZOMBIELAND lies at the bottom of the slope of digi-decline. The Japanese have a word for it – *hikikomori* – a form of severe social withdrawal in teens and young men who become recluses in their parents' homes, unable to go to school or work for months or years.

It's worth stopping to consider the DIGI-DECLINE slope, and where you feature. Honestly? DIGI-ZOMBIELAND is a dark place so if you're there, please seek some professional help.

To help you avoid slipping into *that* territory, here's some information and friendly advice. Soak it up. We figure you're intelligent enough to make whatever changes are necessary because, let's face it, nobody can do it for you.

LAD FACT

Would you rather . . . take a selfie or go swimming with sharks?

Fact: There have been 379 selfie-related deaths in the last 13 years. These include fatal falls from cliffs, accidents with cars and trains, dangerous wildlife encounters and unforeseen drownings.

During the same period, only 90 people have been killed by sharks.

The great re-wiring

We don't want to be overly dramatic but it just so happens that your teenage head is going through what Prof Jonathan Haidt calls 'the great re-wiring'. Your adolescent brain is ready, waiting, wanting . . . *expecting* . . . to reach a new level. It's ready for outdoor, face-to-face, relationship-building, stretching experiences.[94]

It *needs* them!

But of course, if you're glued to a screen for nine hours a day, you're not giving your brain and body the kind of stimulation it needs. Just as neurons that fire together wire together, neurons that *don't* fire together *don't* wire together. If you're NOT having enough personal interaction, your 'how to make eye contact' and 'how to make small talk' neurons will never fire into action. Instead of feeling at ease in society, you can end up feeling socially anxious.

Now, it could be that smartphones are just one more gadget in a long list of technologies that have freaked people out. Telegraphs, telephones, radios, movies, television, video games, even books – all caused panic when they were first introduced, and all have turned out to be less harmful than people feared.

But smartphones really are different. They entice us, talk back at us, nag us, disturb us when we're trying to concentrate, demand our attention and reward us when we give it to them. Worst of all, they're always with us!

Multiple studies have associated the heavy use of smartphones (especially when used for trawling through social media) with negative effects on anxiety,[95,96] self-esteem,[97] empathy[98] and self-image,[99] as well as with sleep problems,[100] stress[101] and depression.[95] Researchers are concluding that smartphones are having a huge impact on the way we (especially teenagers) are interacting – or, rather, *not interacting* – with other real-life human beings.

Sometimes we reach for our phones out of hope or anticipation that there'll be something good waiting for us. But just as often, we reach for our phones to help us avoid something unpleasant, such as boredom or anxiety. It doesn't matter. Once our brains have learned to associate checking our phones with getting a reward, we are going to really, really, *really* want to check our phones. We become like the lab rats, constantly pressing the lever (*gimme gimme*!) to get a pellet of food.[102]

Social media trains your brain to think in ways that are exactly the opposite to what's good for your happiness and wellbeing . It encourages you to be materialistic,[103] judgmental, boastful,[104] petty and negative. Worse still, a phone-based life makes it difficult for people to be fully present with others, even when they're in the same room.[105]

Our basic message is this: if you're in the room, BE in the room. By that, we mean be properly and fully present. Sounds easy, but it isn't.

More often than we'd care to admit, most of us have been trapped in the 'infinite scroll'. Minutes tick into hours and you are well beyond watching the thing that you were actually looking for. The social media algorithms have trapped you in the habit of mindlessly doom scrolling for the sake of it.

Many experts suspect that social media causes our brains to release huge amounts of dopamine (a powerful chemical that can have pleasurable effects) which explains why it's so hard to tear yourself away from your screen. Our brains are *not* designed to be going hell for leather on insanely high dopamine rushes constantly.

The modern brain is running hot!

WEAPONS OF MASS DISTRACTION

When you stop scrolling or gaming, your brain responds to a huge dopamine rush by *reducing* the amount of dopamine in our system. This means that if you binge on social media the levels of dopamine in your brain don't go back to normal afterwards; they actually go *down* to less than normal, because this is how your brain has to compensate for the huge amount it has just been blasted with.[106]

Being low in dopamine makes you tired; it's hard to find the motivation to do *anything*, nothing you usually enjoy seems to give you any pleasure (you know those moments where you can't think of *anything* that you want to do despite having loads of options), and you can even start to feel quite anxious and sad.[107] If this sounds familiar, don't worry. It's not permanent, but it could be a side effect of you spending too long staring at a screen.

No other generation of human beings has ever experienced the 'infinite scroll', so this next bit is a *maybe*. There's a scientific opinion that if you overuse social media as a teenager, you could seriously change the structure of your brains.[108,109] Scientists don't know what this would lead to yet, but some speculate it could permanently affect your ability to concentrate for long periods of time, as you might be *so used* to concentrating in tiny bursts, and it could affect your ability to gain pleasure from things that don't involve screens. It could also affect your ability to connect with other people due to a lack of training of your 'social muscles'. Hence you can choose the perfect emoji but haven't a clue when confronted with a real face!

However, it's not all doom and gloom; your developing brain comes with a positive aspect too. The elasticity that puts you at greater risk from too much social media use also gives you a better ability to recover and change things. Even if, up until now, you've been using social media *a lot,* if you were to seriously cut back, your brain would recover and adapt way faster than an adult brain.[110]

We're not asking you to beat yourself up about your screen habits. Gaming and social media are *designed to be addictive*. We've told you the scary stuff, but we're also telling you that *you* are the person with the power to change it.

Click refresh

SWAP . . .

Reality TV for a walk in the real world.

Procrastination for action.

Online 'friends' for real ones.

Late nights for good quality sleep.

Junk food for fresh food.

Fizz for H_2O

Grumbling for gratitude.

Screen for an active space.

. . . and you'll feel the difference.

Eyeballs for sale

I just googled 'What's the most valuable substance in the world?'
Gold, plutonium, diamonds, rhino horn and saffron are all in there.
But the one that Google missed, the most valuable commodity on the
planet, is . . .

. . . *your attention*!

Here's how the system works. You don't pay for access to the various social
media apps, so you are not the customer. Advertisers pay for them, which
means *you are the product!* More specifically, your *attention* is the product.

It's sometimes called the 'attention economy',[111] because that's what
they're grabbing. Apps are competing for your eyeballs! That's why
online articles contain so many links and there's so much clickbait.

Focus isn't profitable but *distraction is.*

Our phones are designed to get us hooked. You don't see it because it's all you've ever known, but trust me, phones are changing the experience of being human. This is a really big deal because our attention is the most precious thing we have. When we decide to pay attention to something, we are making a broader decision about how we want to spend our lives.

Economists have a phrase, 'opportunity cost' to describe how money could be spent elsewhere. For example, when the government spends £60 million on building a new school, the opportunity cost is that it could have been spent on a new hospital, road or housing estate.

But time also has an opportunity cost. When you spend time doing something, it's at the expense of the other things you *could* have been doing. If you spend five hours a day doing anything, you're going to get pretty good at it. If I spent five hours a day practising the drums, I'd be pretty good within a couple of months. If I spent five hours a day studying Spanish, it wouldn't be long before I'd be able to survive in Madrid.

Pulling all this together, studies show that the ability to create and maintain strong personal relationships is a crucial ingredient in wellbeing .[112] Therefore, the most disturbing aspect of social media and excessive screen time is the effect that it is having on our real-life relationships with other people and as a consequence, on our mental health. Basically, five hours of scrolling is five hours NOT spent chatting, laughing and drinking tea.

Most people sign up for social media accounts out of a desire to feel connected, yet numerous studies suggest that the more we use social media, *the less happy we will be*. Get this – data suggests you're the most digitally connected generation in human history, and also the most lonely, anxious and depressed.[94]

What? Why? *How does that work?*

Because your wellbeing is about establishing *the right kind* of connection. In anthropology, there's something called Dunbar's number which, if you boil it down to the basics, suggests that you spend about 60% of your life with a small circle of 12–15 people. This is your tribe. Your family. Your absolute closest besties. Sure, it's nice to be connected to them by text and phone, but your life is enriched by connecting with them face to face. In fact, the biggest factor in your wellbeing and theirs is the ability to build strong personal relationships with your dearest dozen.[113]

An obvious top tip arises. Work out who's in your 'dearest dozen' and then go spend some time with them. Connect, with earphones out and your phone out of sight, and you too will be the proud owner of strong personal relationships and an amazing life.

Thought experiment

Somewhere in a parallel universe . . .

Wolfgang Amadeus Mozart is a GOAT. Wolfie's up there with Ludwig van Beethoven as one of the world's greatest classical composers.

But let's re-imagine a different outcome if Wolfie had been born in the modern era . . .

Wolfie's mum was stressed to her eyeballs, working three jobs to pay for her son's piano lessons. Her anxiety was born partly from money worries, but more from her son's lack of botheredness. He was loaded with natural talent but Mrs Mozart was at her wits' end trying to motivate him.

'Tea's ready, Wolfie,' she shouted upstairs.

No answer. Guessing he was gaming with headphones on, she texted him.

Again, nothing.

Mrs M huffed in frustration. She took the stairs two at a time and rapped her knuckles on her son's bedroom door.

There were 20 seconds of scrabbling around before he replied, 'What?'

'Your tea's ready love,' she said from behind the door. 'And then your piano teacher will be here.'

'Cancel, Mum. I haven't got time for piano any more. It's too boring. Leave my tea outside the door and I'll scoff it when I've finished this level, or died, whichever comes first. Thanks, Mum. Love you.'

That 'love you' line gives the story a nice touch. Wolfie was a lovely lad, just not bothered. Mrs Mozart did as she was told. Wolfie's pizza and oven chips went cold on a tray outside his room and his piano lessons were cancelled.

Ten years later . . .

The name badge said 'Wolfie', and it had three stars underneath. Wolfie didn't wear the badge with pride; he wore it because he had to. 'Do you want fries with that?' he asked for the 16th time that day.

The switch-cost effect

Here's a BIG thought about the rise of ADHD. If you or your friends have a diagnosis, it's likely to be because you're struggling with something at school – easily bored, distracted, maybe struggling with numbers or reading?

A specialist tells you that your brain is wired differently. Basically, all brains are on a spectrum, and you're at the diagnosable end of it. In the modern day, the expert is merely telling you what you already deep down knew. You acquire the ADHD label to describe your brain 'thing'.

Thirty years ago that was big news. Nowadays? It's fairly standard. It's not your fault. To be fair, you've done well to cope. Once you have a diagnosis, you might be offered some support or meds.

In an earlier chapter we argued that ADHD is not just an individual problem. What if *society* has an attention disorder? What if we've accidentally created a world that messes with your head? We work with plenty of adults who are in a state of daze and distraction, permanently on edge, responding to alerts. But you have it worse! Teenagers are getting an average of 237 alerts a day.[114] Factor in fast food, energy drinks, social media reels, hours of screen time and poor sleep patterns and you have all the ingredients to make your head buzz.

When historians look back at today, I think they'll recognise that we lived through 'the Great Acceleration', an era of warp speed. It's not just technology – everything has speeded up. People talk significantly faster now than they did in the previous millennium.[115] Apparently, we walk 10% faster than we did a couple of decades ago.[116] We listen to podcasts at 1.5 speed. We skip the intro, download one song rather than listen to the entire album, consume five-second videos, use emojis to say how we feel, fast food, next day delivery . . .

It's a fragmented existence. Even our interruptions are interrupted. For example, I'm tapping away at my laptop, writing this book when a message pops up on my phone which takes me to a YouTube video that recommends another video . . .

Meantime, another message has pinged in, so I interrupt my interruption to check the latest interruption, which takes me to an article that my mate says is worth reading. I scroll and accidentally click on something, and I'm lost in a maze of clickbait.

Ninety minutes later I return to the book, but I'm not feeling it. My train of thought is shot to pieces.

This is an example of the 'switch cost effect'.[117] Imagine you're absorbed in your homework and a text arrives. You glance at your phone, literally for two seconds, then you go back to your homework. That's a bigger deal than it sounds. In that moment your brain has been interrupted from its flow state, reconfigured itself to check the text, but then struggles to get back into the zone. You have to remember what you were doing before, and you have to remember what you thought about it, all of which takes a little bit of time and effort. Your performance drops. The switching slows you down. If this is happening constantly, the slowdown is dramatic.

You aren't just losing the three seconds of distraction. You are also losing the time it takes to refocus and get back into the productive zone. It's wasted brain-processing time. All these little costs add up to a big creativity drain.[118]

An American university tested this brain drain by giving students a test. Some had their phones off and others were sent intermittent texts throughout the test. The students who received messages performed on average 20% worse. Other studies in similar scenarios have found even worse outcomes of 30%.[119]

That's a lot of brainpower for a species to lose! The same point, reverse engineered – keep your phone out of sight and your browser focused on the task at hand, and you'll be 30% more efficient, creative and productive.

The virtual you

When you hit teenagehood and you start to really care about fitting in and about your social world, you will almost certainly start investing in your online self. This is the version of you that shows up on social media.

You invest in various platform profiles, making sure each photo is just right before you upload it. You invest in your follower count, in who you do and do not follow; you invest in who you message and what group chats you're in. You invest in talking about what other people have posted online; you invest in making sure all the exciting things that you do are posted on your profile for other people to see.

This online version of us is not real; we never post our boring moments, our six-hour Netflix binges or our homework sessions, only our highlights. We only post the things that we think everyone else will think is cool.

Not everyone reading this book will upload things to social media. Maybe some of you want to but your parents won't let you (cue a lot of anger and longing because of FOMO). You might be a 'lurker' – someone who spends time on social but doesn't post. I guess there's a small chance that you're just not interested in scrolling or screen time at all.

But for those who are posting themselves online, there is one simple question worth considering: why?

Why do you put posts of yourself on social media? Why do you create an online version of yourself to share with other people and engage in all of this online investment?

For quite a few people, the answer will be very simple: *because everybody else does it*.

Humans have always had a sense of belonging. We are pack animals, which means we need to fit into a tribe, clan, family, team or community. The society we live in is essentially a very large tribe and social media has become a huge part of it. Since almost all the celebrities we look up to have social media and post on it frequently, it has become a new form of community interaction.

Because everybody else is uploading their 'best bits' and their highlights, we feel like we need to do the same to prove that we have an epic life too. There is almost this feeling that, if you don't upload it, it didn't happen. The thought of doing something awesome and not letting other people know about it can seem strange.

It's worth pausing to reflect. If we take away the fact that 'everyone else posts on social media', then have a serious think about what reasons are left. Does it make you happy to post on social media? If so, why is that?

In a way, it does make us 'happy'. Seeing other people reacting to what we post makes us feel better temporarily. We feel noticed. It gives us a sense of social validation. The potential issue here is if we start relying too much on

87

other people's online opinion of us. If we start placing too much importance on what people think about us on social media, then social media can become the source of our happiness. But as we all know, social media isn't always 'social'! Your voice can go unheard or, even worse, the reactions can be negative. Followers can un-follow. Friends can un-friend. All of a sudden scrolling has stopped making you happy.

The main person you should be relying on to make yourself happy is you. Not other people on social media, not objects or 'stuff' and not your favourite celebrity. The whole purpose of this book is to help you understand that YOU are the person with the most control over your own happiness and a big part of your personal wellbeing power lies in the choice of how you behave online.

Investing in our online selves takes time and effort. It can be stressful to maintain a steady stream of posts that give the impression that your life is epic, so here is a radical thought – what if we took all the time and effort spent looking like you're having an amazing time and focused it into actually having an amazing life for real.

Dig yourself a media moat

The world has spun a world wide web, and we're the flies. Once you're in it, it's hard to get out. It's what Professor Jonathan Haidt calls the 'collective action problem'. When you rock up at big school you see that a lot of your classmates have got smartphones and are interacting with each other even during class time. That's the stickiness of the web right there. It puts pressure on you to get a smartphone and social media accounts, even though all students would be better off if *none* of them had these things.

The very best parents try to do what's right. If they limit your screen time or suggest you put off getting a phone until you're 10 or 12 or 14 or 16, you resort to stereotypical teenage tantrum behaviour. It's so unfair because all your friends have got phones. You grumble that they're the worst parent in the world when, in actual fact, they're the best.

So even the best parents end up giving in to the collective action problem. They don't want you to be excluded and BOOM, your stroll to school becomes a scroll to school.

Once you've been lulled into the world wide web, it's very sticky. Websites capture so much of your data that they know you better than you know yourself. They learn what you like and what you hate. They know what's on your wish list, what you like to look at, what excites you, what angers you, your triggers and how best to distract you. It's also likely that the algorithms know your date of birth, address, friendship group and where you went on holiday. Armed with that info, they drill down into your attention, trying to capture it for as long as they can. Remember, as far as the websites and social media platforms are concerned, eyeballs equal profit. If they think you might be losing interest, something will pop up.[120]

The algorithm attack dogs get their jaws around your weak spots and sink their teeth in. Blame, shock, anger, clickbait headlines. False claims spread superfast because the algorithms spread outrage faster and further. Outright lies and falsehoods are more sensational than actual real news so that's what they push. As a result, we are being hustled into paying attention to nonsense – things that just aren't so.

Question: What percentage of the water becomes discoloured if you put just a few drops of red dye into a full bathtub of clear water?

The answer is: 100%.

This is what just a tiny amount of anger and hatred does to us. The whole body is contaminated by their presence.

We wish you a clear bathtub and a clear mind.

89

The attention baggers have worked out that in the virtual world, anger is a good emotion. Not good for you *but very good for them!* Anger messes with your ability to think straight. If they can make you angry you'll stop thinking about the poor quality of the argument or whether what you're reading is even true. They've webbed you, and you emerge after 30 minutes of mindless scrolling, angry, frustrated, thinking the world's gone to the dogs.

If you add all these effects together you get the rise of the algorithm and the downgrading of humans. We are becoming less rational, less intelligent, less focused.

I read an article the other day that suggested today's kids are 'cyber-feral children' so here's something that will help tame you.

Have you ever tried to attack a castle? No, me neither, but imagine you were in a medieval army and attacking castles was your job. Arrows raining down from above, the first line of defence was the moat. You'd have struggled into your heavy armour and then have to cross a watery barrier.

The moat was very effective; hence I'm recommending you protect yourself with the modern-day equivalent, a *media* moat. Here are some top tips that range from the obvious to the boring and quirky. They're all undeniably brilliant.

Media moat tips, in no particular order

1. Unfortunately, three quarters of kids aged 6 to 17 go to sleep with their phones.[121] The smartphone has become the modern teddy bear, with a huge cost to energy, attention and success at school. At night, recharge your phone in the kitchen, out of sight, out of mind.
2. Commit to being in the other quarter. No phone or TV in the bedroom. Remember the brain poop page? For a clean, lean, mean thinking machine, treat yourself to lashings of sleep, glorious sleep.
3. Kill the alerts. All of them, stone dead. Switch off all push notifications to your phone and email. Make your screen time an active choice, rather than being a slave to all the buzzing or beeping.

4. Stop taking your phone to the toilet. I'm serious. Going to the bathroom used to be that one guaranteed moment you had to yourself, but now even that has been taken over by the endless entertainment we have at our fingertips. Don't worry, you're not going to miss anything in the time it takes you to squeeze out a number 1 or 2, but you might realise that you have been missing out on a regular opportunity to slow down and be at one with yourself. Toilet time is sacred. It's an opportunity to do your thing and to be 100% present with your body's sensations. Sit. Relax. Smile. *Enjoy!*

5. Detox with a buddy or, even better, with a group. It's easier to be phone-free if you're part of a friendship group who's also 'phone lite'.[122]

6. If you want to continue to stick with vast amounts of social media, you could at least put some effort into changing your algorithm to something more positive. Posting love instead of hate is a good place to start.

7. If you want to go the maverick route, try deleting the apps and see how that makes you feel.

8. Or you could do something else entirely . . . like going outside, taking up a new hobby or putting in the extra effort with that homework that you know deep down you're capable of. Going phone-lite is much easier if you fill the time with something you love doing.

9. Go dark: phones have a setting that allows you to lose the colours. The aim is to make your phone less desirable to pick up.

10. No phones at mealtime. All mealtimes, ever. Messages can wait. Relationships can't.

11. Set aside one day/week to be tech free. From experience, I know this can be difficult, but I've wrestled back a seventh of my life to indulge in non-screen time.

12. Learn to knit. In a month you'll have new mittens and a badly fitting jumper.

13. Instead of checking your phone, do 10 push-ups or squats. You'll be super-fit in no time!

14. Work on your top-secret long-term ambition. While the whole world is scrolling, you'll be powering ahead.

15. Tell people you're making a serious attempt to reduce your screen time. They'll be amazed but also secretly impressed. Six weeks later, when you're buzzing with life, your stress has melted away and you're creating great friendships, they'll join you and, hey presto, *you've become an influencer*!

Give yourself a Niksen break

Who wants less on their mind?

Whilst most of this book has been about giving you a bit of oomph, some get up and go, the top tip from this section is to do less. Our phones have quietly swept in and stolen our peace. They've turned our 'downtime' into 'dopamine-time'. So instead of turning to your smartphone at every available opportunity, our advice is to chill out and give your brain a well-earned Niksen break.

It's a Dutch word which literally means 'deliberately setting out to do nothing'. We love Niksen because it takes 'nothingness' to ninja level. Sitting in a chair, looking out of a window for 10 minutes is an example of the level of nothingness that we're talking about. NOT sitting in a chair scrolling or reading or watching TV. Niksen is diddly squat staring-into-space nothingness.

Give it a go. Guaranteed that you can't do ten minutes of sitting, staring out of your window. It will feel quite weird and uncomfortable after just one minute. If you reach five, it will feel like an eternity. This is because we are *so used* to doing something that we find it hard to just *be*.

If you really struggle with Niksen that's fine! It doesn't mean your brain is broken, just that you're so used to moving at a million miles an hour. We recommend trying a bit of Niksen every day, even if it's only for 30 seconds. Over time it will get easier and easier and eventually you might even start to enjoy it. Your brain will thank you for these quiet moments that help you slow down, and it might even make you less tempted to start reaching for your phone once you're done.

Breaking up with your smartphone

And finally, to nudge you towards becoming a digital minimalist (and life maximiser), here's a letter you should consider writing in your own words:

DEAR SMARTPHONE,

You need to understand that I love you. I always have and I always will. But I'm going to have to walk away, so this is my break-up letter (I did consider writing it as a text message, but that would be too ironic).

We've had such joyous times and shared some amazing videos. And yet somehow, over the past few months something's not felt right. Our relationship's become complicated. *You've* become complicated! Plus, you never leave me alone. All those reminders, emails, notifications and WhatsApp groups. And your constant buzzing. Even in the night!

Cutting to the chase, there's only so long that I can stay in an abusive relationship. My relationship with you has been so full-on that I've neglected the important people in my life. I sit in the same room as them but I'm not *with* them; I'm with you, scrolling, swiping, double-thumbing, liking, poking, commenting, checking, following. And when I'm with you, I'm *absent* from them, which is neither right nor fair.

It's not just at home. When I'm at the cinema, I'm with you, scrolling during the slow bits. I sneak you into lessons, I'm with you on the bus, and we always go to the loo together.

Me and thee, sometimes we can spend a whole eight hours thumb to screen. That's 50% of my entire waking life. And when I'm with you my actual real life is passing by. Recently I started to add up the hours and it made me scared.

Scared of the things I *won't* have done, the sights I didn't see, the moments that passed me by and the people I neglected to spend time with. I need to commit time to the *real* people in my life. The flesh and blood ones. Those closest to me. Those who often sit in the same room as me, thumbing their phones while I thumb you.

I'm breaking up with you so I can commit to them.

So I'm proposing that we cool it. As I said at the outset, it's not lack of love. I love you. I'll always love you, but I need some time and space to get my head together. I'm suggesting we cut down our time together by 75%.

I already know I'll miss you and I'm certain to be tempted so it's got to be mutual. You've got to agree to me switching off *all* notifications and *all* alerts, deleting loads of apps, and . . .

. . . I'm not sure how to say this . . .

. . . we need to sleep in separate bedrooms.

No more between-the-sheets action. That bit's over for good. I know. I'm so sorry. I can actually feel tears welling. You're going to have to agree to sleep on the sofa or in the spare room. You can't be the last thing I see at night and the first thing my bleary eyes lock onto in the morning. It's not healthy.

You say you're all about freedom, but you're not. I feel trapped. You say you're all about connection, but you're not. I feel lonely.

I've got a life that needs living, *fully*. That means I'm truly committed to less *you* time and more *me* time. Because I know that a better me is the key to better relationships with my family and friends.

Thanks for the memories.

X

Chapter 6

REVERSE PSYCHOLOGY

I DON'T KNOW HOW TO BE HAPPY - THEY DIDN'T TEACH IT IN MY SCHOOL.

Chapter Summary

As chapter intros go, this is a weird one. Just go with it and imagine life is like a canary cage.

Some canaries find themselves on the top perch. These birds have a swagger – the best view, the comfiest perch, they can see the blue sky – they sing loud and proud. It's nice up here but there's always the nagging worry that they'll lose their lofty position. These top birds can never settle. They're always worrying that one of the other birds will take their place on the top perch.

Lots of birds live on the middle perches. It's crowded at the halfway point. There's a lot of flapping and pecking and these middle rung canaries are always looking up at the top perch. It sure looks better up there!

And there are some canaries who don't have a perch at all. They're waddling around in the grit tray, being pooped on from above. It's a tough life down here. If you're wading ankle deep through poop for long enough, these birds can forget how to fly!

Okay, so it might not be a perfect analogy, but it does lead us to the point we're trying to make, which is MASSIVE.

Imagine the three levels of canaries in a cage. If you could choose you'd probably say, on the whole, it's probably nicer to be on the top perch. And we'd agree. We could leave the canary analogy right there with the message 'aim to be one of the top canaries on the comfortable perch'.

But the real learning is this: *canaries aren't meant to be caged!* The most 'successful' canaries are the ones who fly freely – presumably in the Canary Islands. These will be the happiest, healthiest birds with the most vibrant colours and loudest songs.

Instead of aiming to be 'top bird', this chapter is about life *outside* of the cage.

Dead calm

I couldn't resist a news feed the other day: *Man Joins Search Party Looking for Himself* took me to a story in Turkey where a man had gone away for the weekend but not told the villagers. When he came back everyone was out in the woods with torches looking for someone. It looked really important so he joined in the search, not knowing that they were looking for him.

It's glorious silliness got me thinking . . . metaphorically, isn't that what we're all doing? Searching. Going round and round in circles, looking for that elusive best self. We catch glimpses, but we never quite catch up. Most people spend their entire life in pursuit of their fleeting amazingness.

This chapter's a biggie because it dares to pose the question: *wouldn't it be great if the search was over?*

To help you step into 'best self' mode, here's a true story from way back.

Several decades ago, aged six, my mum and dad took me on my first ever seaside holiday. The suitcases were packed into the boot of the car and four hours later we rocked up at a caravan in Skegness.

Picture the excitement – my sister and I are running around like cats in a room full of laser pointers while my dad gets busy with the suitcases.

Question for you: how did my dad get the suitcases from the car to the caravan?

Answer: he *carried* them.

He did what? He *carried* them? Is your dad some sort of weirdo? Why didn't he *wheel* them?

Because in those days suitcases didn't have wheels.

Mull that fact around your modern head for a few seconds while it settles. Suitcases have been around for several hundreds of years. Wheels, even longer than that. Suitcases and wheels existed independently of each other for eons, but nobody had ever thought of putting the two inventions together. In fact, if you went to a suitcase shop today and said, 'I'm looking for something *without* wheels' they'd give you a withering look. It makes no sense. Nowadays, every suitcase has wheels. You cannot buy wheelless luggage!

LAD FACT

When the idea for a suitcase with wheels was first proposed, it was rejected because people thought that men would look 'wimpy' if their suitcase had wheels. Even worse, if women had wheely suitcases, they wouldn't need men at all and we'd become redundant.

The point? Until relatively recently, the most obvious combo, the bacon and eggs of travel – suitcases and wheels – had gone ignored.

Park the suitcases and wheels revelation, and I'll come back to it in a minute.

Meantime . . . the study of the human mind has been around since ancient civilisation began but the starting pistol for modern psychology was fired in 1879 when Wilhelm Wundt set up the world's first psychology lab in Leipzig, Germany.

For the next 100 years the field of psychology consisted of a rag-tag bunch of medical doctors, shrinks, geniuses, experimenters and con artists, all doing their own thing. The early days were a bit grim. One of the most infamous chapters in the history of mental health 'treatments' was lobotomy, a truly gruesome 'cure' where a doctor would hammer a medical instrument (similar to an ice-pick) through the top of both eye sockets. This would sever some of the nerves in the brain with the aim of calming the patients down. To be fair, they were a lot calmer afterwards because they could no longer feel any emotions.[123] A pretty big side effect if you ask us.

Thankfully psychology has come a long way since those days.

However . . .

My argument is that despite 150 years of research, no matter how much we spend on therapy, counselling or meds, mental health is getting worse, not better.[124] We won't trot out the stats because we don't need to. You see evidence every single day on the news and in every classroom.[125]

Here's a painful example of where we're at. Recently, I was the guest speaker at an educational conference. I looked out at the 600 people in the audience and said, 'Stand up if you're struggling with your mental health or someone in your family is struggling', and all 600 people got to their feet. I was choked. Either directly or indirectly, the mental health crisis is affecting everyone.

Psychology is now a sophisticated science that has split itself into specialisms. Put your hand up when you've spotted the pattern: *child* psychology looks at children who need help. *Behavioural* psychology looks at ridding people of bad habits. *Clinical* psychology helps people with mental disorders, while *cognitive* psychology is used to develop treatment for mental health problems. *Counselling* psychology is often about marriage break-ups, *grief* psychology is about helping people cope with loss, *developmental* and *educational* psychologies are most often about helping children catch up or manage their ADHD, dyslexia, etc. *Forensic* psychology taps into the minds of the serial killers and paedophiles.

Have you noticed the golden thread?

Yes, these different strands are worthy of study. All are useful and relevant. But they're all aimed at people who are struggling or suffering.

For the best part of 150 years, traditional branches of psychology have been about illness. I've just spent an hour googling the various therapeutic and psychological fields. There are at least 450 different strands of therapy/counselling/psychology, all of which claim to be THE solution. Remedies vary from the NHS-backed therapies that you might have heard of (cognitive behavioural therapy, hypnotherapy and suchlike) to stuff that's a little bit 'out there'. You can experiment with crystals, float in immersion tanks, wet your pants with laughter yoga, or have your eye movements analysed with EMDR (eye movement desensitisation and reprocessing therapy). At the 'way out there' end of the spectrum there's urine therapy (drinking your own wee, or if you don't fancy half a pint of the warm stuff you can massage it into your gums instead) and nude therapy (kind of like 'normal' therapy but conducted starkers in a group).

Most of these theories are well intentioned, but some are definitely more effective than others. At their core they are all about adopting techniques to overcome whatever it is that's bothering you. Although we probably wouldn't recommend drinking a mug of your own pee, no matter how desperate you're feeling.

If these solutions work for you, that's marvellous. The difference in what you're about to read is that it's not about therapy. Or doing. Or learning. Our approach is built on reverse psychology. It's about *being*. And *un*-learning.

Our approach is summarised as this . . . why bother putting you through therapy when, in all likelihood, there's nothing wrong with you in the first place? You're amazing. You might have either just forgotten or become busy doing the wrong things?

It's like wondering why you've got a massive headache without realising you've been clonking yourself on the skull with a mallet. If you're getting by on five hours' sleep, buzzed up on caffeine and sugar, doomscrolling through your downtime, gaming through your night-time, fuelled by fast food, meal deals and energy drinks, it's time to stop innocently harming yourself.

Good news, there is a new addition to the field of psychology. An upstart. Something that's caused a lot of toys to be thrown out of prams by the traditional 'illness-based' psychologies. The bad boy's called *positive* psychology (clue's in the name).

I'm not suggesting I invented it; positive psychology came from America at the start of this millennium, but I'm all over it like a rash. I realised that psychologists had never studied *happy* people on the grounds of them *not being ill,* and all of a sudden it was the most obvious thing in the world. I'd stuck the wheels onto the psychological suitcase.

We can all think of a handful of people in our lives who seem to take life in their stride. These people tend to wear a smile; they have energy, passion and a can-do mentality. They're not rich or famous. They're no cleverer than you or I. They don't have perfect lives but there's a certain 'something' about them. These happy few don't show up on social service's radar or in doctor's surgeries because they feel amazing. Cold-shouldered for too long, I decided to flip psychology on its head and give the happy few a warm embrace. The handful you can think of right now – not only are they happy but they also have the power to light you up too! I sought to answer three simple questions:

1. Who the heck are they?
2. What are the positive outliers doing that enable them to be/stay happier than the majority?
3. What can we learn from them – strategies that we can apply in our own lives so that we might elevate our levels of happiness too?

As we admitted with the suitcases and wheels paragraph, this is a bunch of obvious questions that have somehow been missed since psychology was invented. So that's the backstory. I studied hard and became the UK's first ever 'Dr of Happiness' but if you put the cheesy title to one side, there's never been a more important time to inoculate yourself against the slings and arrows of life.

Clinically happy

Psychology is the study of the human mind. It's epic. If you get a chance to opt for it at college or uni, please do so. All the different strands are interesting, all useful, and all worth studying.

Positive psychology reverse engineers the subject away from 'what's wrong with you?' to 'what's right with you?' Please note, this change of emphasis is quite radical. It's unlikely that child psychologists ever have appointments with kids who are buzzing with vitality, education psychology rarely examines those at the top of the class and forensic psychologists never look into the minds of those who've never dreamed of committing a crime.

Millions are diagnosed as clinically depressed, but nobody has even been diagnosed as clinically happy. Those studies don't exist because, of course, *those people aren't ill.*

So our job was to seek them out, study them and report back so that we might learn the 'secrets' of wellbeing from the ones who are well*beings*.

Here is your ultra-quick win. Having studied human flourishing for 20 years, I can confidently report that happy people live in exactly the same world as you and I. They get homework, it rains on them, their team loses and they have to tidy their room. It became very clear very quickly that happiness was less about what was going on around you and more about your internal processing of those events. Your ultra-quick win is to understand that happiness is an inside job.

Happiness is not an ex-perience; it's an *in*-sperience. Like all other emotions, it takes place in your head.

Get yourself comfy, here's the science bit . . .

If you plotted loads of people on a wellbeing graph (which is basically what I did) it'd look something like this. We've all got an upper and lower level of emotions, and far too many people are spending far too much of their valuable time nestled into the bottom third of the diagram. They don't feel sad, anxious or depressed, just a little bit *meh*.

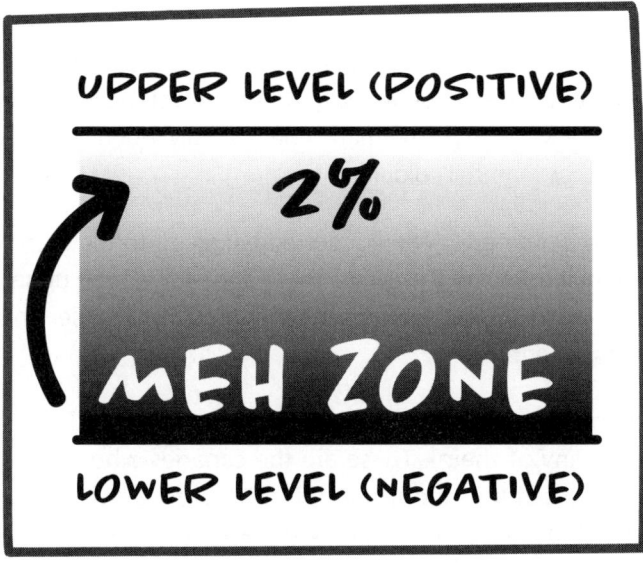

In the same way that vegan cheese hardly resembles cheese at all, the *meh zone* contains very little actual real life! Once the fun, passion, ambition, excitement, love, kindness (etc.) have been sucked out, you're left with blandness. The *meh zone* is characterised by people who are going through the motions. They're alive but not really living.

Look around and you'll see swathes of people suffering from a chronic case of minor glumness. You'll be able to see it in their slouchy body language but most of all you'll hear it, because minor glumness comes with the side effect of low-level grumbling. Some people get stuck in the meh zone and low-level grumbling becomes the soundtrack of their life.

The problem with these conditions is that they're highly contagious. You can be breezing through your day just fine until you're cornered by a minor glumness carrier and wham, you're in total agreement that there's too much homework and you've been sucked into *meh* territory.

Think of it like a zombie virus but without the flesh-eating part.

To be absolutely clear, we are not talking about people with mental illness. That's an entirely different place, below the meh zone. That's not a great place to be and if you're really struggling you need to speak to someone and ask for help. The meh zone is simply when life feels black and white rather than full colour.

But here's the good news. When I plotted people onto the graph I found that not everyone's doing the same. There are a few at the upper end of the wellness graph, a small percentage that are 25% happier and who have 30% more energy.

We call them the two-percenters (on the grounds that there aren't very many of them). These are the canaries who are flying free and this chapter is about them. But before we delve into top tips, it's worth pausing to examine what a two-percenter actually is and *isn't*.

They're normal people, like you and I, but they experience a range of uplifted emotions. They are more likely to feel energetic, positive and enthusiastic, but it's absolutely not about jazz-hands, fakery or being toxic with your positivity. You'll know who your two-percenters are because they're the people who lift you. That said, it's reassuring to know that the two-percenters in my PhD research aren't happy all the time. Just *more* of the time.

People tend to think that *un*happiness is a cause for concern. We're mis-sold the vision that we should be happy all the time. We see other people being uber happy and ultra-successful on their social media 'showreel' without realising it's exactly that – it's for show. It's edited highlights. The reel's not real!

Our industry (positive psychology, self-help, personal development) sometimes gets tangled up in the belief that we should strive to be happy and, indeed, it's a problem if you're not happy! Again, for the record, it's perfectly okay to NOT be happy. My research is proof that even very happy people do have bad days and low emotions.

There's a technical term for this. It's called *being human*.

The trick is something the two-percenters are really good at – knowing how to bounce back.

Click refresh: Two days to change your life

Monday . . . grumble, make excuses, slouch and exist in the meh zone. Monitor how your day goes. How long does double maths feel when you're in half-arsed mode? How do your teacher respond to you? How much progress have you made? On a scale of 1 to 10, how alive have you felt?

Tuesday, come alive. Shine, be grateful, choose a great attitude, own the day. How long does double maths feel when you're in full-assed mode? How does your teacher respond to you? How much progress have you made? On a scale of 1 to 10, how alive have you felt?

Wednesday, compare and contrast. If Monday was epic, rinse and repeat for the rest of your life. It can't be that bad because it's what most people choose. It's the default human setting.

If Tuesday was epic, rinse and repeat. Sure, it requires a little more effort but repeated thousands of times, the rewards in terms of energy, confidence and sheer aliveness are incalculable.

Eye rolling your way to happiness

Whereas everything else in psychology is terrifically complex, the science of happiness and wellbeing sometimes struggles for credibility because it's actually quite simple. But, for the record, 'simple' isn't the same as 'easy'. If it was 'easy' to be living towards the top end of your wellbeing and energy spectrum, everybody would be skipping their way through life, but they're not.

The truth sounds harsh, but it's still the truth. Not everybody gets to be an astronaut when they grow up. Very few get to be footballers or gamers or YouTubers either.

There are a lot of people who are living a dream life, but not in the way they'd hoped. Remember, nightmares are dreams too! Millions are stuck in dead-end jobs, just about making ends meet, kicking happiness into the long grass.

Brilliant lives don't just happen. Stellar careers don't just happen. Superb relationships don't just happen. Happy families don't just happen. Great school grades don't just happen. They all happen because you show up in two-percenter mode *consistently*.

And of course, living the rest of your life as a two-percenter doesn't just happen. It happens because you take personal responsibility for making it happen.

I've spent 20 years studying amazing people and found that being a two-percenter is a set of learned behaviours. They have strategies in place that enable them to flourish.

The biggest strategy also happens to be the most obvious. The stand-out characteristic of people who feel amazing is that they carry a positive attitude with them. Again, think 'simple' but not 'easy'. The two-percenters craft an attitude that works *for* them rather than against them. In my research I call it a 'portable benefit' because once you've learned how to choose a positive attitude it travels with you. Choosing a great attitude seems kind of obvious and yet very few people make the effort required because, let's be blunt, it's a whole lot easier to carry a bad attitude around with you. People gravitate to what's easiest, not what's best!

So, to help you buck the trend, here are a few quick wins that are worth embedding into your everyday.

First up, something ridiculously useful.

You live in the real world which means your day is crammed full of disappointments and minor irritations. So what do we do? We roll our eyes and grumble, *'Why does it always happen to me?'*

Late bus. *No way, not again! And no seats, so I've got to stand up all the way to school. Typical!*

Got to tear yourself away from your screen and eat your tea. Your mum insists on her ridiculous 'no phones at mealtimes' policy. *You're kidding me? Why me? It's just stupid.*

You turn your test paper over and all the stuff you *haven't* revised is staring right back at you. *Aaaagh! Bad stuff always happens to me.*

Another maths lesson that's gone over your head. *Why do I always get such rubbish teachers?*

The alarm clock goes off. You roll your eyes. *Another school day!*

You get the idea. These are all everyday real-world examples that cause us to sigh, huff and mutter under our breath. Let me guess, you and me are alike. You're a magnet for bad stuff, right?

Here's a wonderfully ridiculous top tip that I can personally vouch for. You can keep eye rolling and grumbling that it always happens to you, but only when *good* things unfold.

110

Hear me out: the magic lies in its ridiculousness. Remember, you can keep the eye-rolling and grumbly attitude, but ONLY WHEN THINGS TURN OUT WELL . . .

My bus is on time *again! And plenty of seats. Same as yesterday and the day before. This always seems to happen to me!*

Sitting down with my family to another home-cooked meal. No phones at mealtime. *You're kidding me? Another opportunity to chat to the people I love.*

You turn your test paper over and all the stuff you have revised is right there – *no way! Good stuff keeps showing up.*

Another maths lesson that sinks in! *Why do I always get such amazing teachers?*

The alarm clock rings. Try rolling your eyes and saying, *I'm alive, again! Another school day. Another opportunity to fill my boots with free education! This stuff keeps happening to me!*

Embrace the silliness. You only have to roll your eyes and grumble about good stuff happening to you for a few days before the penny drops and you wake up to the magnificence of your life circumstances. No, the world's not perfect, *but it is amazing.*

You kind of prove it to yourself. You'll be eye-rolling all day long *because good things happen all day long.* The difference is that now you're noticing them.

The positive eye-rolling is reverse psychology that trains you to refocus away from the negative towards the truth . . . good stuff does happen. *Frequently.* Rather than ignoring it, grumbling that it always happens to you reinforces it.

Ridiculous? A little.

Does it work? *Not half!*

Your Get-Out-of-Jail-FREE card

Next up, here's the smallest change that will have the biggest impact on your next 80 years. Steve McDermott came up with the gloriously simple 'four minute rule', which basically basically says that it takes four minutes for other people to catch how YOU feel. So to get yourself and those around you buzzing, all you have to do is be *your best self* for four minutes.

It's like a Get-Out-of-Jail-FREE card because the four-minute rule says you haven't got to be brilliant *all day*, just for the first four minutes of any situation. It kick-starts you and those around you. The first four minutes of coming downstairs in the morning, the first four minutes of each lesson, the first four minutes of sport, homework, lunchtime, coming home from school, visiting your gran – *anything*. If you get the first four minutes right, the rest takes care of itself.

Throw yourself into whatever it is and four minutes later, you'll be buzzing.

Obviously, you've figured out the problem here. You're a teenager, a race of world renowned slow starters. How on earth do you get to be your best self first thing in the morning? You've crawled out of bed, you need a wee, and it's a Monday. None of those factors is particularly favourable.

So here's a bonus tip that helps with those getting out of bed moments. The trick is to *not* have toothache. Let me explain it the opposite way round. Imagine if you *did* have toothache. If you've never had it, I promise you, toothache is proper miserable. It's a nagging pain that won't go away and the only solution is a trip to the dentist, which makes it doubly awful.

'Yay, a trip to the dentist,' said nobody ever.

So every day that *doesn't* happen is brilliant news. Every day you wake up and you *haven't* got toothache is a wonderful start to the day, which will put you in a fabulous mood. That means you'll be feeling amazing so by the time you've had your wee, got your school uniform on and made your way downstairs you will be bursting with positivity from *not* having toothache. That means your first four minutes of family interaction is positive rather than 'grumpy teen' and remember, the first four minutes is all it takes.

Oh, and if one day you do have toothache, pick another body part. If your kidneys are working, your heart's still beating and your skin's still waterproof, celebrate one or all of those instead.

Warning – it's very easy to do the total opposite of the four-minute rule. It's easy to spread early morning grumpiness. It boils down to making a little bit of effort with your attitudinal choice.

16/10/6: Pass it on . . .

Here's another interesting and incredibly simple idea. The world is plagued by screen zombies. People are engaging with the virtual world but neglecting those around them. In terms of engaging with your fellow flesh-and-blooders, try using one more sentence than you would normally. Push yourself to engage, just a smidge, and instead of a standard one-line answer, up your game and offer something extra.

When your mum asks you, 'How was school?' rather than brush her off with a teenage shrug or 'Boring', 'Fine' or 'Please stop asking!' upgrade to one more sentence. For example . . .

If you want to keep the stereotype you can play it low key and go for 'Mostly boring but with a cracking lunchtime. And how was your day, Mum?'

Or you could lose the stereotype and go upbeat. 'Yep, it was pretty good, thanks for asking. We did this amazing thing in science today. . .' and share your highlight.

Again, it's your call. But one more sentence gives you a better chance of actually engaging with the people closest to you. In a world of *disengagement*, you'll stand out a mile and make your mum proud.

One final sciencey piece that's well worth knowing is that your happiness is bigger than you. When you're in two-percenter mode you create a 16%, 10% and 6% emotional ripple effect that reaches three degrees of people removed from you.

This means anyone you meet will catch your happiness by a minimum of 16%. Plain simple English? Your family, friend and teachers will all catch your happiness – but it doesn't stop there. Your teacher is 16% happier (because you've been a joy to have in class and she's caught your happiness) and she goes home to her family. Her family is now 10% happier (you haven't met your teacher's family, but it's your happiness they're feeling).

But your happiness virus doesn't stop there either! Let's assume your teacher's teenage son then pops out to the supermarket to buy some milk. He's 10% happier, so has a bit of banter with the lady at the checkout, and she's now 6% happier. And, no, you've not been anywhere near the supermarket.

So your happiness contagion has spread to your teacher by 16%, to her family by 10% and to the checkout operator by 6%. And, of course, you're creating this happiness ripple with everyone you meet.

Bottom line, if you can't be bothered to wear a great attitude for yourself, do it for those around you. They'll appreciate the uplift in their lives.

The Jonah complex

In all the time I was doing the two-percenter research, I was puzzled as to why so many people get stuck in the *meh* zone. To be honest, I spent about 40 years there myself, but why?

Being in the two-percenter zone is so easy and the benefits are completely life changing. There is literally no downside to you raising your wellbeing bar from mental health to mental WEALTH. Plus, there's nothing fake about it. The two-percenters research isn't about teaching you to be like everyone else or trying to be someone you're not. It's about encouraging you to be more of *who you already are at your best*.

So why on earth do so many of us end up hating Mondays, counting down to weekends and struggling with our energy and positivity? The truth falls in line with everything else in *LADULT* – it's deadly simple. Cutting to the chase, the reason we don't live our best lives is because it's easier *not* to. Let's explain by the little-known but super-powerful Jonah complex.

We're all birthed into this world in the same way – naked and screaming! Someone cuts the umbilical cord, the midwife rubs a sponge over you, wraps you in a towel and hands you to your mum. She smiles down at you, you try to fix your blurry eyes on her, and it's love at first sight. There's a bond and, fingers crossed, that's the start of what psychologists call a secure attachment.

Wind yourself back to that moment. At one hour old you are a mass of pure potential.

The possibilities are endless. You, *one hour old*, with your whole life stretched out before you, it's knee-shakingly exciting to imagine what you could achieve.

Hey, it's not just you. At one hour old, we all have unimaginable potential.

And then, all too soon, vast numbers of humans reach the point of wishing they could get a mirror with a better view. What happened to all that potential? All that stuff the person in the mirror *could* have done and all those things I *could* have achieved . . . why does my reflection look and feel so average?

A lot of this failure to live up to your full potential can be explained by what's called the Jonah complex. Long story short, Jonah is a guy from the Abrahamic scriptures who got famous by being swallowed by a whale. But Jonah's less well-known claim to fame is that God asked him for a big favour, and he declined. He was a humble market trader, a fairly normal bloke, and thought it was too big an ask when God wanted him to up his game. Jonah refused. 'Go ask someone else, boss. I'm just a humble market trader'. (I'm guessing; I wasn't there.) He preferred to play small.

He now lends his name to the Jonah complex which suggests the reason that we don't achieve greatness, the reason we don't fulfil our potential, the reason we don't live in the two-percenter zone, is not that we can't, but that we *daren't*.[126]

We're running scared of our own greatness! Although we talk a good talk about 'living our best life' and 'being our best self', we're in love with the *idea* but spooked by the *reality* of it. It might be too daunting to be stand-out amazing. If I come to school with a grin on my face, people will think I'm a weirdo. What if it's too difficult to be my best self, or what if I try to raise my personal bar and fail? If all my friends are kind of coasting, it's a bit risky to be seen to be working my butt off.

The Jonah complex means we end up standing in our own shadow. It's easier to fit in rather than stand out so we talk ourselves down from the heady heights of being a two-percenter.

FEAR

↑
IT'S JUST A TINY WORD!

I have no idea whether the Jonah complex holds any water for you personally, but the fear of our own greatness is a point well worth considering because it suggests the biggest thing stopping you from shining is you.

If the possibility of being remarkable shoots a thunderbolt of fear into you, here's something to consider. Looping back to the fact that life's a short and precious gift (remember, no re-spawns), what's the point of aiming for mediocre? If life is a one-time-only offer, why would we settle for middle of the pack? Why would you set an average bar for being a teenager, friend, son, brother, grandson, nephew, next-door neighbour or pupil?

When the truth is that you're much better than that!

Here are three massive points that jump out from the Jonah complex. Your potential won't unfold by accident. It reveals itself through, firstly, knowing it's there, secondly, making a conscious decision to tap into it and, thirdly, consistently pushing yourself to test where the boundaries are.

That's what the world needs, and while you can't command anyone else, you can lead by example. So instead of waiting and waiting (and waiting and waiting) for someone else to take the lead, do what the two-percenters do and step forward.

Chapter 7

BE A NICE MAMMAL

Chapter Summary

Switch on the news and you'll see there's a world shortage of niceness. Angry people have taken over the world. There's a lot of shouting, violence and rabble rousing. Which is why we've devoted a whole chunk of *LADULT* to the simple act of kindness.

But to make it interesting we've created a pyramid and provided a step-by-step climbing guide. All the levels are great, but we reserve a special place for level four where your kindness leaks out into the universe.

We think it's a beautiful chapter.

Enjoy!

The hierarchy of human kind

The vast majority of people are absolutely lovely. Eyes on their phones, walking into lamp posts . . . but lovely.

Some are a bit less nice. They might be stuck in some sort of life situation that has sucked the loveliness out of them but you know their prickliness is temporary. We all have times when the milk of human kindness feels semi-skimmed.

Then there's the rest of them, the handful who seem perpetually angry with the world, with their not-so-niceness spilling over into society. Whereas old fashioned trolls used to live under bridges and hassle Billy goats, modern day trolls have evolved into a social media menace. They hurl abuse, tear people down and criticise.

So here's something for everyone. It's a pyramid, much smaller than its Egyptian cousins but bigger in terms of everyday usefulness. Welcome to the hierarchy of human kind. See you at the top . . .

Level 1: Be kind to yourself

It's common knowledge that you can't pour from an empty cup. In human terms, you cannot give what you haven't got, so kindness needs to start close to home.

Very close! Kindness starts with *you* being nice to *you*.

It seems like an obvious place to start but, funnily enough, this is the level that people struggle with the most! We all have an inner critic, a nagging voice of self-doubt that provides a running commentary about how rubbish we are.

The problem with the inner critic is that every cell in your body is listening in on your inner dialogue. It just so happens that life deals you loads of situations to beat yourself up about, so switch the narrative, catch yourself doing things well, give yourself a bit of encouragement and compliment yourself on a situation well handled.

It gives your pyramid of human kindness a firm grounding because it's *you* learning to be your own best mate.

Click Refresh

There will always be a critic. There will always be someone who puts you down. Don't let it be you.

Level 2: Be kind to your future self (right now)

This level is about self-care and, in particular, making choices that your *future* self will thank you for. That sentence needs a bit of unpicking . . .

It boils down to this: the best thing you will ever do for the people around you is take really good care of yourself. That might sound selfish but it's actually the least selfish thing you will ever do. The people you share your life with need *you* fizzing with energy, enthusiasm and positivity.

Taking it into the future is where self-care gets immensely powerful. I've become better at looking after myself now (in this moment) while also keeping a lookout for the wellbeing of my *future* self. So, basically, I've got an eye on my health and happiness tomorrow, next week, next month and next year.

Yes, it's a bit spooky, but *today's* me is looking out for the *future* me.

For example, you've had a tough day at school so you might seek to relax with 20 minutes of screen time *(one episode or game can't hurt surely?)*. Before you know it, 20 minutes has morphed into three hours, and one episode has expanded into half a season. Although that might feel good right now, it's not being kind to tomorrow's self; the you who is groggy, sleep deprived and with their homework still undone.

Level two of the pyramid has no problem with the 20 minutes of screen time but if you've got one eye on the wellbeing of your *future self*, 20 minutes really is 20 minutes. The rest of the evening is a combo of things that will help your *future* self flourish – homework, guitar, football, reading, time with family . . . whatever it takes to prime yourself for a great day tomorrow.

Rocking up at school bright eyed, bushy tailed, healthy breakfasted, homework nailed. That's level two, right there.

Be aware, this is about a thousand times more powerful than it sounds when you read it off a page. Having a right good go at looking after yourself now (in this moment) while also keeping an eye on the wellbeing of your *future* self means things that you used to find difficult – eating healthy food, getting good sleep, looking after your fitness, knuckling down in lessons – all of a sudden become a whole lot easier. There's a future version of you that will thank you for the choices you're making today.

Level two of the pyramid hints at this: *don't let the future you down!*

Level 3: Random acts of kindness

If levels one and two are about filling your own kindness bucket, level three is about spillage.

Science (and common sense) tells us that the quickest way to feel amazing is to do a good deed for someone else. Random acts of kindness can range from a smile, a chat, holding a door open, making someone a cuppa, telling someone they're ace, giving a hug, cleaning up a mess, holding a hand, paying a compliment, thanking your teacher for an amazing lesson, etc. The point being, they're totally random. You didn't plan them. There was an opportunity for kindness *and you took it*.

Hey, I'm not sure how to say this without it sounding critical, so I'll just blurt the truth . . . a lot of the older generation have a negative view of the youth of today. They see gangs on the news, they read about stabbings, they see litter, they hear swearing and they feel threatened.

Hence why a random act of kindness *from a teenage boy* will break the stereotype and make their jaws drop. You help someone by reaching to the top shelf in the supermarket, you hold a door open, you smile and say 'Hi,' you use your manners, you see litter and pick it up . . . people will see these things and they'll tell everyone what they've seen. Young people nowadays . . . *aren't they amazing!*

So go ahead punk; make someone's day.

Level 4: Be kind to things

Definition

'Stuffocation': drowning in possessions

Kindness extends beyond people, to animals, property and your environment, including old Mother Earth herself.

She's been kind enough to provide us with a delicate ecosystem. We're in the Goldilocks zone, just far enough from the sun not to burn alive but close enough for warmth. Just the right gaseous mixture to create breathable air. Just enough of an ozone layer to protect against deadly solar radiation. This big bang of local circumstances has enabled millions of species of flora, fauna and life to co-exist. But it's a very delicate balance.[127]

If you want proof that intelligent species exist in other galaxies, here's your evidence . . . they're intelligent enough to stay away from humans. This last century has seen us take a wrecking ball to our planet. Our relationship with Mother Earth is that we're takers, not givers. As a species, we're single handedly altering the planet's chemical, biological and physical balance.

It's safe to say that if people got wiped out, all other species would benefit enormously. With the human wrecking ball gone, the biosphere would breathe a sigh of relief (literally!). Forests would regenerate, oceans would clean themselves, fish stocks would recover, the air would purify and orangutans would move into our deserted tower blocks.

I'm not asking you to take personal responsibility for all of it, but level four of the pyramid asks you to do your bit. Again, this is easier said than done because the global party lights are flashing and, hey, who can resist a Golden Ticket to the materialist party?

A thought about money

Just to be clear, if you plot income and happiness on a graph, at no point does having more money make you *less* happy. So while it's *technically* true that money can't buy happiness, it can buy choice, comfort and airline tickets to somewhere with palm trees.

Money doesn't guarantee happiness, but it sure helps smooth the way. 'Stuff' will bring you instant but short-lived happiness. It can also bring debt. To squeeze more value from your happiness pound, spend it on experiences.

Or, if you want to buy a 'thing,' buy something that helps you have an experience (a bike, skateboard, new pair of rugby boots, tennis racket, festival ticket).

Today's world makes us feel like we are not enough because we don't *have* enough. If you haven't got a smartphone, you want one. If you've got one, you want a smarter one. If yours is already super-smart, you want a nicer phone case. The prevailing thinking is that *once you have got enough, then you'll be content*, hence the vast majority are chasing more stuff in the hope that it'll bring them some inner peace.

It's called musterbation (note, with a 'u'). This is when you turn things you'd quite like to have into things you ABSOLUTELY MUST HAVE! You're lured in by some wonderful advertising, so you buy whatever product it happens to be and, guess what, you do feel amazing. Sometimes for a whole hour! And then there's another advert with another shiny happy person, even shinier and happier than the previous one, and he's got a different product. That must be what you need.

No wonder everyone's exhausted, we're musterbating like mad! (again, still with a 'u')

But look around and ask yourself, is it working? Does everyone look super happy? Is everyone living their best life? Or are they just in a never-ending chase?

Exactly!

Rather than accepting the golden ticket and joining the party that's dancing itself to death, we think there's a better alternative.

The solution? Instead of changing the climate outside, why not change it inside with peace, contentment and a bit of spiritual enlightenment. The enlightened woo-woo bit begins with a massive shift of thinking. *Once you've got enough, then you'll be content* never works, because you'll never have enough. It pays to switch the sentence to the slightly weird truth, which reads, *once you're content, you'll have enough.*

> **Click refresh**
>
> Social comparison is difficult to switch off, so use it to your advantage by comparing downwards if you want to feel lucky and upwards to feel driven.

To switch off your want-ometer (and to massively reduce your desire to musterbate, yes, still with a 'u') you need to learn to be satisfied with what you already have and who you already are.

That requires a big dollop of gratitude, so here is your two-step homework.

Step one, you need to write a list of 30 things that you really appreciate but take for granted. Phrased differently, what 30 things or people are you lucky to have in your life but might have taken your eye off?

Anything goes. Mine would include clean drinking water, oranges, trees, vegetable samosas, warm showers, memories, pencil sharpeners, being British, *Toy Story 2*, music, the smell of autumn, oxygen, British grass (if you've ever trodden on Spanish grass you'll know what I mean), white blood cells, fresh coffee, homemade jam, walls with moss on, a frosty morning and my mountain bike.

Most people spend a massive amount of their time grumbling about what they *haven't* got, whereas your list of 30 should prod you in the opposite direction. Step two, go through your list one by one, allowing yourself a few seconds to focus on each item. Linger just long enough so the feeling of gratitude squirms right down into your stomach.

Please note, this activity is borrowed from actual therapy. It's tried and tested. Thinking about what you're grateful for each day and taking the time to write those things down is the best homework ever because it gives headspace to each one. It means the great things in your life won't just pass you by anymore. You'll notice them. And you'll realise that, even if you've had the toughest of days, you've actually got a fair amount of good stuff and nice people in your life.

As you keep practising, you'll learn more about what brings you joy, so you can start focusing your time and energy on the things that make you the happiest and best version of yourself.

Click refresh

Ask yourself:

www: what went well?

ebi: even better if?

Level 5: Be kind to the unkind

Brace yourself; in fact, you might need to sit down before absorbing this one. It's super advanced, high-level, nosebleed kindness territory.

No matter how kind you are, there will always be unkind people. I'm guessing that when kindness was being handed out, some people were at the back of the queue and there was none left. In the olden days, haters might have whispered behind your back or had a grumble in their head, but now they can tap away at a keyboard and spit negativity at anyone and everyone.

It's worth mentioning that it's usually hurt people who hurt people. The trolls will always be there. We aren't saying you have to praise them for being unkind, but your attack dog tagline should be this: if you can't beat 'em, definitely don't join 'em.

Stay hygienic[1]

Someone just posted a really hateful comment on my social media feed. I don't see the man who made the comment as a 'hater' or any other similar label. In fact I don't see him at all because he's gone . . .

. . . comment deleted. Person blocked.

Remember the order: Delete – Block – Let Go – Move On.

Never reply.

Your head will be screaming to retaliate. But when you pick their s*** up and throw it back, you end up with *their* s*** on *your* hands.

You're better than that.

Stay hygienic.

Our level 5 challenge to you is this; if you're going to earn the kindness black belt, you have to be super-kind to *everyone*. Yes, even the one or two unkind people who don't seem to deserve it. If they're not very nice people, that's because they've not experienced enough kindness or love.

---

[1] *Thanks Richard Wilkins*

So to reach the top of the pyramid of human kind, you have to love the unloved, be nice to the not-so-nice and be kind to the unkind. That gets you to level six, the peak of kindness, a fully paid-up member of 'human kind'. We're thinking of getting some badges and T-shirts done?

It all points to this: be a go-giver as well as a go-getter. In a world that is dominated by differences, let kindness be your religion.

Paws for thought[2]

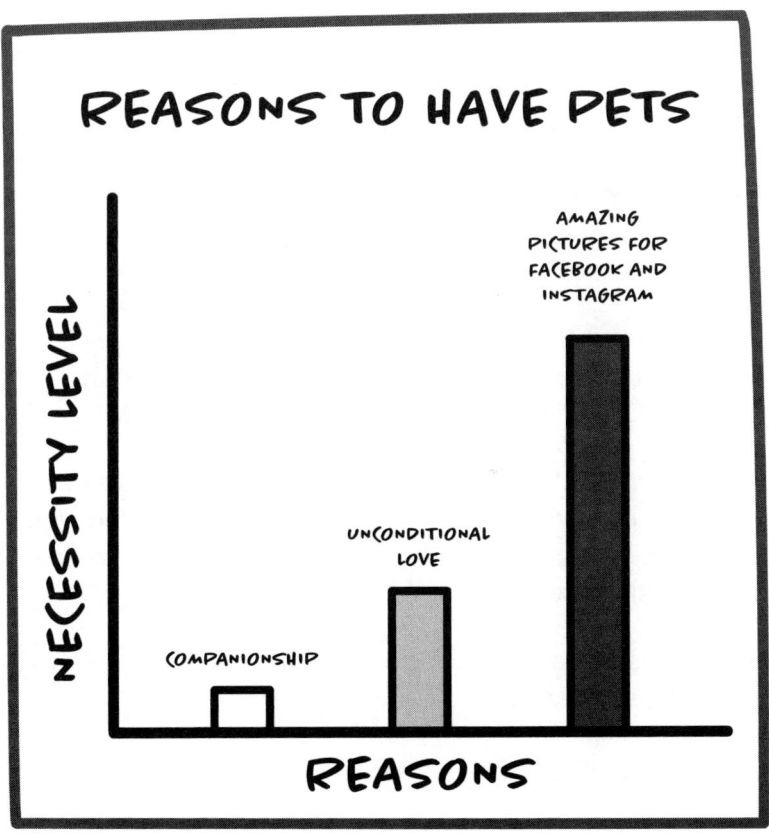

---

[2] Adapted from Fred Craddock, "But What About the Weeds?" in *The Cherry Log Sermons* (Louisville: Westminster John Knox Press, 2001).

We ummed and ahhed about this chapter ending. It was written, binned, re-written and binned again. Because, obviously, boys wouldn't want to read an imaginary story about a conversation with a dog.

But what if the story had a meaning that cemented the chapter themes together? A BIG meaning. A meaning that wasn't spelt out, but that they had to work out for themselves? So right at the last minute, it was back in. . .

I once had an imaginary conversation with a dog. It was deep, and it went like this . . .

I have never been to the greyhound races, but I have seen them on television. They have these amazing dogs, wearing snazzy jackets, who chase a mechanical rabbit around the track. When the dogs get to the point that they can no longer race, the owners put a little ad on greyhound.com to see if anybody wants to adopt one for a pet. If no one takes them, the dogs are destroyed.

My Uncle Geoff can't stand the thought of the greyhounds being destroyed, so he adopts them. He has several of these big old greyhound dogs hanging around his very small house. Geoff loves them.

Once, when I was at Uncle Geoff's, a big spotted greyhound called Charlie was lying there in his basket. One of the kids in the family, just a toddler, was pulling on Charlie's tail, and a slightly older kid had his head on the big dog's rib cage, using it for a pillow.

Charlie didn't seem to mind. In fact, despite being tormented, he was wearing a big satisfied doggy smile.

I said to Charlie, 'You still racing mate?'

'Nah,' the dog said. 'Gave it up.'

'Do you miss the glitter and excitement of the track?' I asked.

Charlie lifted his head to look at me. 'Not at all,' he said.

'Why did you stop? Did you get too old to race?'

'Gosh no, I had plenty more racing in me.'

'Well, what then? Weren't you winning?'

'I was UK champ three years on the bounce. I won over a million pounds for my owner.'

'Well, what was it then? You can't just give up. Was it bad treatment?'

'Oh, no,' Charlie replied. 'They treated us royally when we were racing.'

'Must have been an injury then?' I guessed.

'Nope. Fit as a flea.'

I was puzzled. 'Then why?' I pressed. 'Why did you stop racing?'

'I already told you,' smiled Charlie. 'I quit.'

'You quit?'

'Bingo,' said the dog. 'Simple as that. I quit.'

'But why did you quit?'

'I discovered that what I was chasing was not really a rabbit, and I quit. All that chasing, all that lung-busting running, and what was I chasing? It wasn't even real.'

Charlie put his head back down so that he could be a better pillow for the little boy.

Chapter 8

WELCOME TO THE PLEASURE DOME[1]

---
[1]*Some parents pre-read books for their kids to check that the content is suitable. If you're one of those parents, thank you for caring. But you might stumble at this chapter. It might seem that pornography is a chapter too far. You might think your son doesn't need to know or that he's so sweet and innocent that he'd never access naughty websites. In which case, we'd respectfully suggest that you're wrong on both counts. Sadly, the average age at which boys access pornography is eight years old. Remember, this chapter isn't written for parents; it's written for the boys themselves. Do your son a huge favour and let him decide whether this chapter is important or not. Thank you.*

133

Chapter Summary

Welcome to a quick and dirty chapter about something quick and dirty that affects every teenage boy. Like moths drawn to a light, you'll be seduced by porn. Single-handedly (excuse the pun), pornography has taken over the world. You literally can't avoid it because, rather than you seeking it out, porn's chasing you down. You can run, but you can't hide. The availability and variety are dazzling.

We start with a quick history lesson (plot spoiler: it's all the fault of the Danish), compare the sex lives of bonobo chimps, pandas and porcupines, before venturing into an informative, no-nonsense account of the industry in all its messy, degrading, eye-popping, addictive glory.

Rather than sweeping this difficult issue under the carpet, we tell it as it is. From then on, it's up to you.

I spy, with my little eye, something beginning with 'p'

Admission time: this has been a tricky chapter to write because there are a couple of elephants in the room. So let's out them . . .

The first is masturbation. There – shock, horror – we've said it!

For the record, masturbation is not a crime and, although nobody wants to talk about it, everyone does it. Some people go old school and use their imagination, but these days many lads find it more satisfying if there are some visual aids. A prompt or two to get you in the mood.

Which brings us to the other elephant in the room, the p-word, pornography. There – shock, horror again – we've gone and said another taboo word! Why? Because instead of sweeping these issues under the carpet, we need to have an informed discussion about them.

Opinions are split. Pornography can be any combo of exciting, hilarious, offensive, thrilling, unpleasant, dirty, degrading or disturbing. But one thing's for sure, there's a lot of it!

A generation ago, young men had to seek out pornography. Now it seeks you out. The modern world is serving up lashings of porn in various styles and flavours. There's something for every taste and, for some people, this can be highly addictive.

Of course, there's a small chance that you've never come across it yet, but we felt morally obliged to include it in *LADULT* due to how many teenagers are now accessing it. In fact, it's so common that a recent study,[128] which was trying to compare the brains of young men who'd never watched porn with the brains of young men who had, found that they couldn't get enough people for their study. Specifically, the researchers couldn't find *any* young men who hadn't watched pornography. Not a single one.

Quick backstory – naughty pictures have been around since art has been around. Some fairly hardcore drawings of people having sex can be traced back to ancient Mesopotamia, which was 3,000 years ago.[129]

As soon as the motion picture was invented in 1895, some directors began making sexually explicit (for the time) videos and realised that the controversy they stirred up meant there was money to be made.[130]

In 1969, Denmark officially became the first country to decriminalise pornography, leading to other countries following suit, and a significant and dramatic increase in production.[131] This stuff was starting to look more like the pornography of today: full colour videos of people getting it on.

But video technology in the late 20th century was archaic by today's standards. Back then, it was on video tapes, a physical product that had to be bought and sold. Also you had to go through the embarrassment of going into an adult video store or asking the guy in the regular video store to go to his 'special cupboard', all for the pleasure of watching a grainy video of a man and woman 'doing it'.

Boy, how the world has moved on. Nowadays, it's not just a man and woman. Anything goes. And the porn industry has cut out the need to visit the store and suffer the embarrassment of handing over your cash for something in a brown paper bag. Nowadays the best and worst of human sexual endeavour is beamed direct to your eyeballs. It's widely available, much of it's free, and with a non-stop stream of new content, it now seems to be a widely accepted social norm that teenage boys will just go through a phase where they're obsessed with porn and are constantly beating their privates into submission.

So why is that? Why do some young men find it so hard to look away? And should we be worried about this new social norm? Unsurprisingly, it comes back to testosterone and that inner caveman. In most young lads, puberty and the adolescence that follows lead to a huge surge in hormones and a significant spike in sexual arousal.[132]

It won't happen to absolutely everyone, and different boys might get the hormone surge at different times, but most teenage lads live in a state of sexual readiness. It's not something that you can do a great deal about. Testosterone pulses through your veins and, hey presto, you feel horny. All of a sudden one day, either by word of mouth or by accident, you start enjoying yourself and your usage of Kleenex has quadrupled.

Rewind once more. In the wild, hunter-gatherers didn't live that long, so the sooner a young male was ready to get it on, the better it was for the tribe. It was quite simple. Back then most humans had two aims: firstly to stay alive and secondly to stay alive long enough to reproduce. Sex is a critical part of natural selection, so we've evolved to absolutely love it. And I mean, *really love it*.

Sex is a natural thing but here's where humans differ from most other animals. Unlike other species where they might have a lot of sex very quickly during a mating season, humans can have sex all year round and are one of the only species on earth that have sex *for fun*.

This is almost unique. It's basically just us and bonobo chimps, our closest living relative.[133] Lions, for example, don't mate for fun.[134] Neither, to the best of our knowledge, do porcupines. *Ouch!* Famously, pandas struggle to mate at all.[135]

Bonobos are even worse than us! They have sex all the time. They use it to say hello, goodbye, sorry, thank you and 'your hair looks nice today' among many other things.[133] If a human were to act like a bonobo, we would probably send them to see a doctor and to be diagnosed as a nymphomaniac, the official term for a sex addict.

Given that a lot of humans love sex *almost* as much as bonobos, it means that sex is also very important for us, and therefore natural selection has made it borderline impossible to resist.

And of course, pornography taps into this human weakness by appealing to our deep primal sexual instinct. The nucleus accumbens is your brain's pleasure centre, buried deep into your primitive wiring, and porn makes it buzz.[136] When we do stuff that we really enjoy like eating, laughing, exercising and of course sex, the nucleus accumbens gets hit with a big surge of dopamine which feels . . . *amazing*.[137] The pleasure surge is designed to be moreish because it helped our ancestors (and us) repeat the behaviours we need to repeat in order to survive.

But it has a dark side: when things really stimulate this part of the brain, it can become addictive. Psychologists call it hedonism: the pursuit of instant gratification. Food (especially sugar), alcohol, drugs, gambling – these are all examples of things that are addictive thanks to the pleasure circuit, and all things where an addiction to them can have real negative consequences on someone's health and life.[138]

But over the past decade, research into addiction has revealed that internet porn may be on this list as well and that it may be especially addictive and damaging to the teenage brain.[139]

> I asked the doctor whether masturbation causes poor eyesight.
> He said, 'You're in Aldi, mate!'

Porn has morphed into a very big industry, run by a mix of exploitative but clever people and people making films from their bedrooms. Unlike the old days when you had to spend money for one or two porn videos, which you'd quickly get bored of, porn websites are full of novelty; the constant stream of new videos to click on and open gives the brain a never-ending source of fresh things to trigger the pleasure circuit.[140] This combines with the fact that porn appeals to our deep, evolutionary liking for sex, and all of a sudden the pleasure circuit is in overdrive! This is why porn can be super addictive, especially when timed with the monumental surge in hormones that teenage boys go through. In a sentence that's never been written in the English language before, you are the perfect porn storm.[141]

Porn is what we call a 'supernormal stimulus', which basically means it's something that is more extreme or exaggerated than we would find in nature, which makes us respond more strongly than we normally would. Science tested this in birds by taking some mother birds who had just laid eggs and putting them in a cage with a choice: their freshly laid eggs or a set of fake eggs that were bigger and more colourful than the eggs they would find in the wild. Horrifyingly, the mother birds chose to incubate the big, colourful eggs instead of their real babies. The fake eggs' size and colour were so exaggerated that the mother birds' brains went into overdrive, and scientists believe that porn may work in a similar way on us.[142]

So far, we've told you what you already know – pornography is hard to NOT look at. But coffee is addictive and that's not damaging my life, so here comes the 'so what, now what?' bit.

More and more young men have been appearing in doctors' surgeries with erectile dysfunction. This is a problem traditionally faced by men who are much older, where the penis can no longer get hard enough to have sex. But recently, an increasing number of *young* men have been coming to the doctors with 'porn-induced erectile dysfunction'. The difference with a lot of these new cases is that their penis works perfectly fine when they use internet porn but doesn't perform when they're with a real person, even if that person is someone they really fancy![143]

Some young men find that they can only have sex with their partner if they're watching porn at the same time. While we admire male multitasking, it's a very sad state of affairs if you reach the point where your man equipment isn't up to it.

Obviously, we don't want that to happen to you. We have no idea where you are in your sexual development but, plot spoiler, sex, *in a loving relationship with a real person*, is the best thing ever.

If you trace the problem back to source, lots of these unfortunate cases involve guys who start watching internet porn as teenagers. Then they progressively watch more variety, including some hardcore stuff, and end up experiencing sexual dysfunction during what should be their 'peak years'.[144]

Teenage brains are incredible; they're very 'plastic', which means they can develop to adapt to whatever they're learning or doing really well. If your brain is constantly being stimulated from the heady combo of novelty and nakedness, it will adapt to become really, *really* good at getting pleasure from internet porn.[145]

Quite simply, neurons that fire together wire together. The neurons branch out, creating connections and pathways. If you're not careful, what feels like an innocent habit of watching some sneaky soft porn every now and again is your brain's gateway drug into much harder stuff.

In plain, simple English, the brain becomes amazing at responding to porn, making it less adapted to real life. It can lead you down a slippery slope of bad mental health outcomes including social anxiety and the inability to form high-quality relationships with real people.

Now obviously not *everyone* who watches internet pornography becomes addicted (most don't in fact), some people never get close, and some might be 'sort of addicted' for a bit then grow out of it. It could also be that we're scaremongering? Maybe we're making a big fuss over a bit of porn and surely it's just a case of boys being boys?

Possibly, *but no*.

Because although loving sexual intercourse between two consenting people is perfectly natural, porn is 100% NOT natural.

General intimacy, handholding, kissing, skin-to-skin contact and of course *real* sex. That's incredibly natural.

But how much of this do we see in pornography? Not many lads are going to log on to watch some adults holding hands. Porn is filmed in order to record as much of the genital contact as possible while minimising everything else, which leads to our 'actors' having sex in bizarre contortionist positions so that none of the rest of their body gets in the way. This feels pretty rubbish and is comically unnatural, which those of you reading this will realise when you get to experience sex for the first time.

Sex is all about skin-to-skin, face-to-face contact, as well as smells, sounds (not like the comically loud moaning you hear in porn) and a whole host of other sensations. The positions you end up in would make for a *terrible* porno shoot, so I think it's fair to say we can stop considering fantasising yourself into porn scenarios as 'natural'.

Porn can lead to unrealistic expectations of sex and yet it's pretty much everyone's first exposure to it. This is where the real danger lurks. Lads can get some pretty warped ideas about what sex actually is or involves. It can lead to young couples, where one or both parties have watched a lot of internet porn, trying or doing things they aren't comfortable doing just because they think that's what they should be doing from internet porn. Equally problematic, boys can sometimes force girls into doing things they've seen on screen.

To be clear, that is an absolute no-no. Even in the height of sexual arousal, 'No' means no, 'Hands off' means hands off and 'Stop' means stop. Always. Forever. No exceptions.

To finish this difficult section with some clarity, we're not shaming anyone who has used, currently uses or is thinking of using internet porn. There's an inevitability about it. We're just telling you straight and trusting that the messages have landed. What you do from here is up to you. Pornography isn't inherently evil. It exists in such vast quantities because there's huge demand. It's also easy to use it negatively and destructively but, equally, it's perfectly possible to use it sensibly and responsibly.

The ball's in your court.

Chapter 9

LADS GET SAD TOO

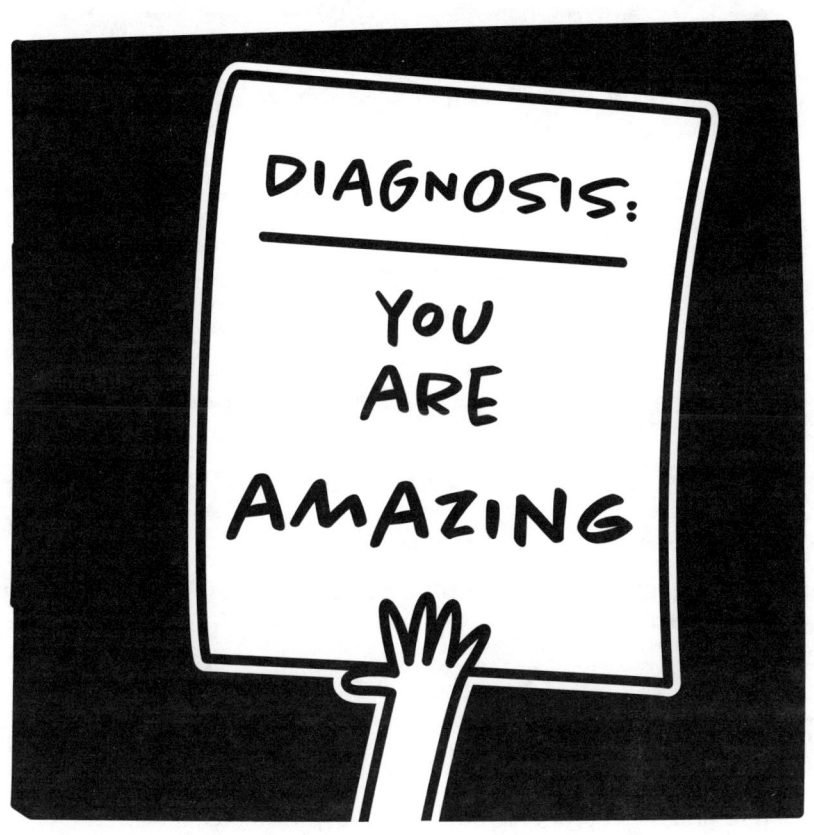

Chapter Summary

If you want to take down a werewolf, a silver bullet will usually *do* the trick. But there aren't silver bullets for anything else. There's no *one best way* to motivate, be happy, feel confident or truly live. There's also no silver bullet for resilience or mental health.

However, there's something very close. The only long-lasting permanent solution that will upgrade you from mental health to mental WEALTH is peace of mind. So here's our mental health chapter that, fingers crossed, is absolutely NOT what you're expecting.

You'll be surprised what you can learn from a Newcastle United footballer and bamboozled when we suggest a mild touch of neurodiversity might be just what the doctor ordered. We compare life to the most boring bit of the funfair before introducing some revelations from Finland and Japan and bagging some learning from zebras in Africa.

Your reward for hanging in there is to feast your eyeballs on our chapter finale – a big resilience message heavily disguised as a silly story about a cuddly toy called Perdy.

But first, here's the insane story about the hardest man you've never heard of . . .

#ToughestGeezer

I used to find myself cringing at footballers' post-match interviews. They'd trot out the same 'Sick as a parrot', 'Over the moon' and 'It was a game of two halves' clichés, but the biggest teeth-grinder was when a player explained that he'd given 110%. Or occasionally 120%. A Newcastle United footballer once suggested the team had performed 360% better in the second half.

On reflection, that might be utter genius?

Anyhow, my teeth were grinding away because you can't give more than 100%. Basically, if you give a task *everything you've got*, that's 100% you've given. A 100% is your absolute maximum.

But then I learned about Adrian Paul Ghislain Carton de Wiart and if humble pie had calories, I'd be morbidly obese. Footballers, I salute you. You absolutely can give more than 100%.

De Wiart was a British Army officer who fought in some meaty battles (Boer War, First World War, and Second World War), gathering a Victoria Cross and a whole load of letters after his name (VC, KBE, CB, CMG, DSO). We've no idea what those letters mean, but there are a lot of them. They look impressive and signify that you've got balls of steel.

Described as 'the soldier who wouldn't die', if social media had been around in his day, de Wiart would surely have been #ToughestGeezer. His military history reads like a who's who of near-death experiences. He was shot in the face, head, stomach, ankle, leg, hip and ear; was blinded in his left eye; survived two plane crashes; and tore off his own severely injured fingers when a doctor refused to amputate them.

Yes, you read that right – *he tore them off!*

You'd think he'd slip into retirement but, oh no, not #ToughestGeezer. Despite being too old and battered to fight in the Second World War, he fancied one last scrap so signed up anyway! He was captured and imprisoned in a concentration camp where he made five escape attempts, including seven months of tunnelling (with one arm and one eye).

On the one time he did escape, de Wiart evaded capture for eight days disguised as an Italian peasant (note, he was in northern Italy, could not speak Italian, and was 62 years old, with an eye patch, one empty sleeve and multiple injuries and scars. That's hardly 'blending in').

And here is the best bit about #ToughestGeezer: describing his experiences, de Wiart wrote, 'Frankly, I enjoyed the wars.'[146]

Hey look, there's resilience and there's Adrian Paul Ghislain Carton de Wiart Resilience, with a capital 'R'. We're not advocating that you sign up to be shot at, that you rip your own fingers off, or that you spend the next seven months tunnelling from the school toilets to the high street . . . but de Wiart's extremes of resilience back in the day lead us into a discussion about resilience in the here and now.

Lads' war facts

1. The shortest war in history lasted 38 minutes. It was between Britain and Zanzibar on 27 August 1896. Britain fired a few rounds, the Zanzibarians surrendered, shook hands, job done.[147]
2. In Liechtenstein's last military encounter, they sent 80 men to fight and 81 returned because they'd made a friend.[148]
3. In 1788, the Austrian army managed to fight itself. After a mix-up involving drunken soldiers and a language barrier, they mistook each other for the enemy, leading to chaos and significant casualties.[149]
4. We all know people can get worked up about a footy game, but how about a war? In 1969, the South American countries of Honduras and El Salvador went to war for a few days after a particularly tense World Cup qualifying match.[150]

Sisu

Here's a wonderfully short word that packs a big punch: *sisu*. Pronounced *SEE*-su, it's a word from Finland that doesn't quite translate into English. *Sisu* relates to the psychological strength that allows a person to overcome extraordinary challenges. When you're running on empty and you're not sure you can carry on, *sisu* is your emergency 'reserve tank' that somehow keeps you going. The closest we have in English is grit, bravery, fortitude or resilience.[151]

But sisu runs way deeper than that. #ToughestGeezer, he had bags of *sisu*. In fact, he's proof that you can probably have too much sisu!

For us mere mortals, it's about the fundamental understanding that the best helping hands are at the end of your own arms. *Sisu* helps YOU help YOU when YOU need help the most. It's about digging in.

It's more than a word. *Sisu* encapsulates an entire philosophy. It's almost a middle finger up to the toughest times in your life. *Ha, thought you could break me? Think again!*

Note, sisu isn't really about the day-to-day trials and tribulations of life. Everybody has homework pressures, relationship issues and rainy days. Embedded in *sisu* is the fundamental truth that life is punctuated by *major* challenges. *Sisu* is about embracing tough times and thanking them for making you stronger. Best of all, it's about building character.

I doubt Adrian Paul Ghislain Carton de Wiart knew the word *sisu*, but he was living it for sure. We're not suggesting you compete with #ToughestGeezer, but rather that you squeeze every last drop of learning from the old boy. Remember, when it was all over, the one-eyed, one-armed, no-fingers, bullet-holed war veteran is quoted as saying, *'Frankly, I rather enjoyed the wars.'*

It'd be nice for you to reach 110 years old, reflect on your ups and downs, and be able to say, in all honesty, *'Frankly, I rather enjoyed my life.'*

The cliché-ridden footballers were right all along. You *can* give 110% if you end up giving *more* than you thought you had. *Sisu* is potent because it helps people *exceed* their known capabilities.

The remainder of this chapter is about tapping into your own sisu. But anxiety and mental health are thorny issues, so before we wade into the swamp, it's worth looking at what resilience *isn't*.

Firstly, for clarification, resilience is not about being shot at or ripping your own fingers off. That's stupidity.

Second, your father and son tag team couldn't be any clearer when we say that lads get sad and *real* men DO cry. It's what makes them real. Sometimes life throws so much adversity that it's perfectly natural to have a big sob. Over time, you begin to master your emotions, but right now, in the midst of growing up, the pressures can cause a meltdown. Crying is your safety valve. It changes the climate in your head by letting some internal weather leak out through your eyeballs.

Pretending you're okay when you're not – that's not resilience either, it's fake. Bottling things up sets you up for trouble further down the line when pressure gets too much and the bottle explodes.

Other things that resilience *isn't*: it's not about putting a positive spin on things, or denying your fear. It's not even about developing mental toughness. Not *really*. Being resilient doesn't mean that you'll never feel scared or insecure, or that you should stay in a situation that doesn't feel right.

When people talk about 'becoming more resilient', they're all about learning tools and techniques that will make them more battle-hardy.

Whereas what we're about to talk about is subtly (but hugely) different.

Resilient is what you already are.

It's a pre-existing quality, factory-fitted into all human beings.
Dr Ann Masten calls it 'ordinary magic'. It's your true nature. Once you understand how the human being truly operates, you will be tons more resilient, because you will feel safe to immerse yourself in the ups and downs of life.

That's the journey we're taking you on, via the African savannah . . .

Think like a zebra

Silly question #1: What does a fly, a mouse, giraffe, squirrel, zebra and *you* have in common? Other than good looks, obviously.

They've all got something called a Hox gene, which acts as a kind of template instruction for how the animal should develop. Wildly different animals have the same genes, so the Hox acts as a genetic instruction manual that sets out roughly where a fly's legs, wings and head should be. Same with you, but without the wings.[152]

That means we all came from the same Hox – a long-extinct ancestor that has been preserved for ever in all of us.[153]

Silly question #2: If we have more or less the same DNA as a mouse, why can't a mouse, say, invent a new type of cheese? Or, instead of waiting (and waiting and waiting) for their long necks to evolve, why didn't giraffes invent step ladders? Why haven't squirrels invented a FindYourNuts app? As for monkeys, what can I say? They share 95% of our DNA yet can't even make a decent cup of tea.

That's because they're all missing the *missing link* – an evolutionary brain adaptation that's allowed humans to rule the world.

We'll explain by moving from silly questions to a silly fact: did you know that zebras don't get stomach ulcers? That's because they haven't got a pre-frontal cortex – that's the chunk of brain above your eyebrows. If you put both hands to your head as you would if your team concedes a last-minute goal, your pre-frontal cortex is exactly that bit (it also comes with an anguished facial expression; you know the one).

If a zebra's team conceded a last-minute goal, it wouldn't put its hooves to its head because it hasn't got a pre-frontal cortex, hence no capacity to experience anguish. I can't help thinking – lucky zebra!

The pre-frontal cortex is a relatively recent neurological upgrade that allows humans to reflect on the past, to dream about the future, to make plans and, best of all, to imagine things that aren't there.[154] To the best of our knowledge, zebras don't reminisce about the good old days or count down to the weekend.

This thinking upgrade is amazing, but also a curse because it means our brains are large enough to torment us. Let me explain, sticking with the medium of stripey horses.

Imagine a zebra, tail swishing, head down, munching on the grasslands of the African savannah. Always alert, the zebra spies a lion springing from the long grass. Adrenaline kicks in and the zebra legs it, running faster than it knew it could, until it manages to outrun the lion. The big cat slinks back to the long grass, mane ruffled and tummy rumbling, and within 60 seconds of feeling safe, our chubby black and white horse will resume its tail swishing, head down, chomping away at the grass. The lion is gone. Panic over. Done and dusted. Move on.

Now, just for a moment, imagine that you're on holiday somewhere in the African savannah and you catch sight of a lion emerging from the long grass. It's prowling. The zebra has escaped its jaws, so it's doubly determined to get a tasty steak – a human rump. You drop your phone and run faster and further than you thought possible. Eventually, lungs busting and sweat patches merging into each other, you lean against a tree and mop your brow. It's been a near-death experience, but you've escaped. *Phew!*

You'd return home, traumatised. You'd visit your GP and be prescribed something for your anxiety and panic attacks. Your brain would replay the 'lion incident' over and over again, waking you up with 3am cold sweats. You'd have time off school with a diagnosed 'big cat phobia' and wildlife documentaries would cause traumatic flashbacks. Over time, this consistent anxiety causes acid in your stomach, and you'll get an ulcer.

150

Zebra: no neo-cortex, no ability to over-think, no excess stomach acid, fine and dandy.

You: neo-cortex, massive ability to over-think, PTSD, stress hormone flows around your body, stomach ache, ulcer, surgery.

So the human brain is a magnificent piece of kit that's allowed us to take over the world, but it's come at a price. Medics call it somatic disease, where our mind affects our body. Our ability to think causes us to literally be worried sick.[155]

Here's where it gets really unfair. Criticism, insults, rejections, mockery and failure – these events create a rush of the stress hormone cortisol,[156] which assaults our sense of self-worth, especially if done publicly. Your brain processes it, and it stings like hell.

But nice things, such as receiving praise, acceptance and winning, also produce a neurological reaction, the warm glow of oxytocin which conjures pleasure and pride.[157]

But chemically, these hormones aren't equal. Oxytocin (the nice warm glowing stuff) is removed from your bloodstream in about five minutes, whereas cortisol (the jagged, edgy chemical) can linger for a couple of hours.[158]

It means the good feelings get washed away while painful ones linger. It's unfair, but biology is what it is.

The key point about our zebra section is the mind-body communication system – somatic illness – that your *thoughts* affect your physical body.

Let's bank that knowledge and go up a gear . . .

Beyond diagnosis

A quick word about the various neurodiverse conditions – dyspraxia, dyslexia, dyscalculia, ADHD, autism spectrum disorder and suchlike. You might be carrying one of the labels. If you're not, you'll know loads of lads who are because in your lifetime, they've sky-rocketed.

To be clear, you are NOT your diagnosis! Your diagnosis tells me where you're at, not who you are. If you really want a diagnosis (and a lot of people do!) here's one for you: you are amazing. You are a miracle. You're a walking, talking, breathing, experiencing machine.

Every condition has a spectrum, from 'worst-case scenario' at the tough end to 'you've got it, but you'll be perfectly fine' at the not-so-bad end.

We'll start with the tough end because it's important to recognise how difficult these conditions can be for many people, and the simple truth is that, for some, their diagnoses are not a superpower. People on the tough end of the diagnosis spectrum are people who need care and supervision for their entire lives, and who often can't do basic things without some help. They can still live long and happy lives, but there's no point sugar-coating it; it can be tough sometimes on them and the people who care for them.

At the not-so-bad end, the various neurodiverse conditions are less life-altering and more like a different operating system. They're hurdles that you can learn to overcome. In fact, quite often, they're super-powers that you can learn to harness.

The human brain is continually resculpting itself. If there's a setback in one area, it compensates elsewhere. Autism, for example, is associated with the struggle to tune into facial expressions and tone of voice[159] but can be compensated with extraordinary laser-like focus and attention to detail.[160]

Teenagers diagnosed with dyslexia might struggle with the written word, but the brain often compensates with creativity, speed of thought and novel solutions.[161]

Here are a few famous names. Spot the ink:

Environmental campaigner, Greta Thunberg.[162]
Pop star, Billie Eilish.[163]
Former England captain, Sir David Beckham.[164]
Business guru, Sir Richard Branson.[165]

The pattern? Asperger's, Tourette's, OCD and dyslexia, respectively. They've all done rather well for themselves not *despite* having a neurodiverse condition but most probably *because* of it. They've had to adapt, think differently and develop a skill set that made them incredibly valuable.

Some tech companies are even *deliberately* seeking out employees with autism because of their attention to detail and skill set.[166] So, if you are in possession of a neurodiverse label, instead of it holding you back and defining you, it could be your path to an incredibly bright future. Just as LGBTQ+ is about diversity of physical and sexual differences, we should be accepting and celebrating neurological differences as part of human diversity.

Click 'Refresh'

The 10-year rule

Bad grade? Awkward moment? Embarrassing mistake? You won't even remember most of these in a few years. Learn from it, move on, and don't waste energy on temporary problems. The rule of thumb is that if it won't matter in 10 years, don't waste 10 minutes stressing about it. Don't sweat the small stuff (and almost everything is small stuff).

WHAT IT SEEMED LIKE:

WHAT IT WAS:

■ THE END OF THE WORLD

■ UNPLEASANT
■ A LESSON TO BE LEARNED

Snow globe thinking

In terms of resilience, what most people are talking about is 'acquired' resilience – tips and tricks that will toughen you up. But we're talking about *innate* resilience. *Built-in* resilience. And that's a subtle but crucial distinction because the only long-lasting, permanent solution that will eradicate mental illness is peace of mind.

In terms of challenging prevailing wisdom, I'm going to pick an argument with traditional thinking. Let's imagine that you picked up a major footballing injury. It wasn't anybody's fault but a crunching 50:50 tackle broke your leg.

I think we can all agree that's not ideal.

I'll tell you what happens next. The ref blows, the game's abandoned and they cover you up in tracksuits and coats to keep you warm while they wait three hours for an ambulance. The professionals in high-vis jackets cart you off to hospital, where you get fitted with one of those new-fangled leg casts, with Velcro. You hobble around for about eight weeks, revisit the hospital, get checked over, and are good to go.

The body is amazing. You leave your injured leg well alone and it fixes itself, good as new.

What you absolutely don't do is return home from hospital with your freshly broken leg, rip open the Velcro, remove the cast and attempt to re-enact the tackle. If you were stupid enough to do that, it'd be horrifically painful and you'd make the break worse. If you removed the cast every week and re-did the tackle, your leg would re-break and re-break and re-break. It'd never have chance to fix itself and you'd be in hellish pain forever.

Our point? Your physical body, if left alone, will normally find a way to heal itself.

So let's move the same argument to your mental state and, in particular, your thinking. More often than not, the running commentary in your head keeps going back to bad places: regrets, embarrassing moments, failures, shame and critical remarks. In actual fact, most of the professionals working in mental health will also metaphorically re-break your leg. You're actively encouraged to tell the school counsellor (nurse, psychologist, social worker) about all the things that have gone wrong in your life. Your mum and dad's break-up, a death in the family, a traumatic memory . . . *what happened, how do you feel* . . . by retelling the incident, you're re-living it again and again and again . . .

It's like going in the shower to dry off. *It ain't working!*

Whereas, quite often, if your thinking is left well alone it'll correct itself. It's like a snow globe. Sure, there are times when your world has been shaken and things are stormy, but those times pass and calm is restored.

Honestly, nobody reaches the ripe old age of 30 without experiencing some sort of major trauma. A relationship break-up, the death of a loved one, an exam catastrophe, a major illness – you name it; if it's not happened to you yet, it will.

That's not doom and gloom, just fact.

There was nothing wrong with finding these events truly painful, and it is absolutely helpful to talk about your feelings with others. But dwelling on them, re-living them again and again – that bit needs to change. What you need to do is change your relationship with your thoughts. You need to learn 'distress tolerance', to sit with embarrassing, sad or angry thoughts without fighting them or inflaming them.

We're not designed to re-live our traumas. We're designed to learn from our traumas and move on. It's called post-traumatic GROWTH, and the next section hints at how.

Your script

We all have what are called 'trademark behaviours' – the things that are you, through and through.

The problem arises when your trademark behaviours are working against you. People are innocently harming their life chances by continually getting in their own way. We see it all the time in adults but it also shows up (big time) in teenagers. Habits like answering back, showing lack of respect, eye-rolling, doing the bare minimum – these are all classic self-defeating teenage behaviours.

It pays to step out of your own shadow by replacing them with *positive* trademark behaviours. Which brings us to the deadly word: change. Humans like familiarity, so once a habit is grooved in it can be tricky to un-groove it.[167]

Take a big breath; we're going deep.

Behaviour follows from your ego which, if you remember, is your identity. You behave according to who you *think* you are.

Your thinking acts as a script, telling you what role you should be playing in life. Written in first person, your script tells you what to say and how you should act. The audio version plays in your head. It's the running commentary. Most people's scripts are quite critical and the vast majority follow the script. They spend their entire life thinking it's accurate and true. And most people cope just fine. They get used to the negative commentary in their head and are perfectly okay. But if life is a one-time opportunity, and you're intent on taking it by storm, 'fine' and 'okay' set the bar very low.

Learning some new lines for your script is a good start. Telling yourself a better story will get you surface-level change. So, for example, telling yourself that you're a hero rather than a villain is a decent way to change your life's story. But to rise out of ordinary into extra-ordinary, you need to understand that the script isn't real. The running commentary in your head is all made up. And YOU are the maker-upper!

We can't control all our thoughts, and sometimes thoughts will appear which will make you think, 'Where on earth did that come from?'. This is normal, and it doesn't mean something is going wrong. We're talking about an overall theme change in the script inside your head, particularly of the ones you *do* control.

The script has massive implications. It means people are anxious so much of the time because the world they're creating inside their heads is such a dangerous place.

Our *LADULT* argument is that the modern world is pretty cool, but change has accelerated to cheek-wobbling warp speed. Our brains can be over-stimulated and buzzed up on the wrong messages. The script is messy. People are running scared of their thoughts.

Top tip: *don't believe everything you think!*

NOW *o'clock*

A woman told me the other day that her life was a rollercoaster. So I cast my mind back to my last encounter with a rollercoaster just to see if the analogy fits. It was called The Big One at Blackpool. You might know it. In case not, let me paint a picture. It's a slow start as you *click-clack-click-clack- click-clack-click* upwards, your heart already thumping because you know what's coming . . . you arrive at the crest with no time to enjoy the sea view before you're plunged down. It's very down, and very fast. And down some more.

Then there are ups and downs and twisty-turny, stomach churning, eye bulging, loop-the-loops. You scream your way through more twists as the loose change falls from your pocket and you swallow your fillings. And then comes the all-too-sudden rudeness of the finish. Anchors on, your car comes to a rather sudden halt, the weight is lifted from your shoulders and you step out, wobbly legs, green around the gills, hair everywhere. 'Oh my gosh, that's the scariest thing ever. Never again!'

There's excited laughter and 60 seconds later you've joined the back of the queue for another go at the 'never again' rollercoaster.

If she meant *that* rollercoaster, then I'm properly jealous. Her life is one hell of a ride!

But it got me thinking, is life really like that?

If my life was likened to a funfair, it'd be more hook-a-duck. Sure, I have rollercoaster days with twisty-turny bits that make me want to scream, but those days are in the minority. They're the punctuations. There are long stretches of hook-a-duck where not much happens. I can wave my arms around and pretend but, on reflection, my life's busy, but quite ordinary. There's a lot of sitting in traffic, there are meetings, online nowadays, most of which are a bit dull. And some Netflix. There's a lot of me waiting for my toast to pop up. I wait in line at the supermarket, I send emails, water the plants, feed the cat, do the washing-up, brush my teeth, put my socks on . . .

Honestly, I'm a best-selling author, doctor of happiness and international keynote speaker, yet my day-to-day is quite ordinary.

Happiness means finding a moment of joy in those ordinary moments. Because those moments add up to hours . . . and those hours add up to life itself. It boils down to this – if my life is mostly hook-a-duck with occasional rollercoaster rides thrown in, it makes sense to learn to be happy in the quiet moments. Because the waiting for toast to pop up, brushing my teeth and virtual meetings are in the majority.

These quiet moments *are* my life.

Guessing they're your life too?

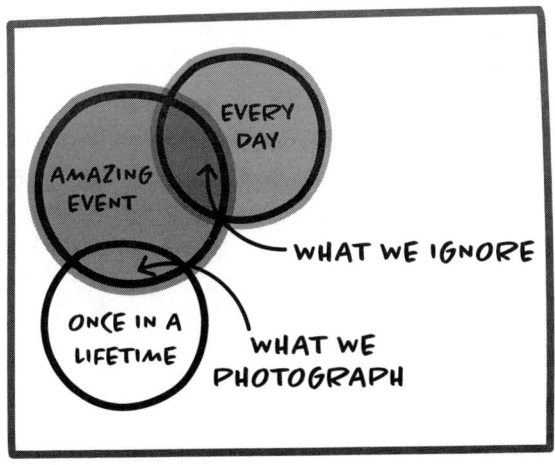

Which brings us to the uber-sexy subject of mindfulness and its drop-dead gorgeous cousin, meditation. We're told to live in the moment but which moment? There are so many of them!

Well actually, no. There is only ever one moment. It's called 'now' and it's right here. It always has been and it always will be. The present moment is always available. It's always here. The question is, where are you?

It's a half-decent guess that, more often than not, your moments will be spent doing stuff: scrolling, texting, walking, talking, drawing, writing, playing, eating . . .

You've become a human doing instead of a human *being*. Mindfulness is about *being* in the only moment there ever is, which is the one you're in right now. Your entire life is played out in the present moment.

Yes, it's kind of weird but I promise you it's true. Let me prove it. Let's take last weekend as an example. I'm sure it was wonderful. You can probably remember what you did and how you felt. But you can only remember last weekend from right now. It's almost as though 'right now' is a kind of science fiction wormhole that allows you to access the past and future.

The same principle applies to the future. The wonderful weekend you're looking forward to – when you reach the 'future', that will also turn out to be your present moment.

This is another of those hang-on-to-your-pants moments because the big reveal is that if your entire life is lived in one moment (called 'NOW'), then it makes perfect sense to fall in love with now.

> Guilt lives in the past. Worry lives in the future. Peace lives in the present.
>
> – James Clear, author

But if sitting cross-legged on a gluten-free cushion isn't your thing, here's a simple mindfulness hack all the way from Japan. Originating from 16th-century tea ceremonies, *ichi-go ichi-e* literally translates as 'for this time only' and also as 'in this moment, an opportunity'.

Ichi-go ichi-e recognises that everything we experience is a unique treasure that will never be repeated in the same way again. So, for example, on the surface, a cup of tea with your family might seem like an everyday occasion, but each gathering is a unique experience. The exact same people having a cup of tea tomorrow will create a different atmosphere.

Without wanting to sound too new age, becoming aware of *ichi-go ichi-e* helps me take my foot off the accelerator and remember that each morning I spend in the world, every moment I spend with my wife and children is infinitely valuable and deserves my full attention.

Even better, awareness of *ichi-go ichi-e* means I feel much less weighed down by the past or anxious about the future. It's a super-clever form of mindfulness that leaves you smiling inside.

Ichi-go ichi-e runs deep because the human brain is really good at time travelling. It remembers all your mistakes from your past and stresses you out about a scary and unpredictable future, all the time missing the only moment there ever is, which is THIS ONE. Once the penny drops that there is no past or future as such (they're both images created in the present moment in your head, they are not real), and that it's always NOW o'clock, *ichi-go ichi-e* is your Golden Ticket into the present moment.

Oh, and please don't expect every moment to be an all-singing, all-dancing party. Life's not like that. Hopefully, one day you'll meet the love of your life and have an amazing wedding. That special day will be a full-on extravaganza, but the 70 years of marriage that follow will have lots of routine, boring bits.

Life is made up, even for the most exceptional people, of vast swathes of ordinariness. We humans spend much of our time sleeping, eating, sitting on the toilet, walking, waiting for buses, sitting on buses, chatting with friends, answering texts, scrolling, cleaning our teeth, showering, looking at screens, visiting relatives, watching mediocre TV . . .

Most of the 8 billion human inhabitants of planet earth live unexceptional lives, and even the exceptional ones are filled with vast periods of unexceptional moments. So rather than coming alive in the amazing moments, it pays to flip the view of what an amazing moment is. *Ichi-go ichi-e* helps you see the beauty in all the things you do in between the exceptional moments.

Not every day is amazing, but there's amazingness in every day. You don't need to filter life, or yourself, just look at it through *ichi-go ichi-e* eyes.

The truth fairy

Warning, this next bit is all about cuddly toys. But if you're a young man who thinks they're too cool for silly stories about cuddly toys, *think again*. One of our biggest revelations is hidden beneath the fabric.

Cast your mind back to when you were five years old. You probably had quite a few cuddly toys, but there will have been one or two special ones.

Ollie had a soft spot for a giant stuffed dalmatian called Perdita. Perdita was great for snuggling up to in bed, but even better when used as an opponent in a wrestling match. After probably thousands of body slams over the years, Perdita isn't looking her best, but that didn't make the younger Ollie love her any less.

For many this 'special toy' would be a cuddly toy, because you'd often have it with you when you went to bed. It's that toy that your parents would give you when you were really upset, because a cuddle with *that* toy would make everything better. It's the toy that you'd get in a panic about if you couldn't find it, and the one that you'd even take on holiday. This toy was your favourite because it made you feel safe, secure, and loved.

Here's a horrifying thought. If you were to take Perdita, or *your* favourite childhood toy, and cut into it with a knife, what would you find? Ripping open our favourite childhood cuddly toy would be quite traumatic, but we guarantee that you'd find absolutely no love, safety or magic comforting ingredient. Nope, your favourite cuddly toy is most likely filled with 100% stuffing, no love included, not even one percent.

Which leads to an obvious question. If our most cherished stuffed toys are just stuffing, then where do our feelings of love and comfort come from? Here's the breaking news: 100% of those feelings of love, comfort, safety and happiness, they are all coming from *within* us. As children we may feel as though those feelings come from the toys, but in reality they're all generated from within.

We used your favourite cuddly toy as an example, as we get older we keep doing exactly the same. We move on from cuddly toys and start attaching our emotions to other things: school assignments deadlines, someone un-liking us on social media, parents nagging us, a new haircut, video games, a hug from our crush, a rainy Monday, a sunny Wednesday, 3.30 on Friday . . . the list goes on.

It really seems as though all of these things make us feel in certain ways, when in reality, our feelings come from us. We aren't feeling the outside world, we are *feeling* whatever it is we *think* about it.

Here's the truth, in a nutshell: You are feeling your thinking. You can never have a feeling without first having a thought.

So here's a big thought: If every feeling you ever experience is coming from your thinking, and your thinking is mostly negative. . . anger, frustration, anxiety, worry, panic, a sense of being on edge – THAT'S WHAT YOU'LL BE FEELING!

The breakthrough is when you realise your emotions are less to do with what's going on around you, and more to do with what's going on inside you. Emotions work from the inside out!

Yes, we know that it's a complete reversal of how life appears to you. It absolutely looks as though your grumpy mood is coming from Monday, or your joy is fed and watered by 4pm on Friday – it seems that way to us too. But it's a trick of the mind. You are, in fact, *feeling* your thinking in this moment. *Always*.

Let's take an example: exam nerves. How can anxiety from an exam next month time travel from the future to make you nervous right now? The truth is that it can't! Those feelings of nervousness don't come *from* the exams, they come from how you think about the exams *in this moment*. You can apply this to so many situations: crushes, social anxiety, sports games, whatever. The answer will always be the same.

We aren't telling you this so that you can become a complete master of your mind. The truth is that we can't control *all* of the thoughts that we ever have, our brains are very complicated. We're telling you so that you know how the human emotional system truly operates – from the inside-out rather than outside-in.

As this understanding sinks in, the world will start to feel a little lighter. It won't be perfect, but you'll be carrying less of a burden in your head. With less on your mind, you'll experience a calmer, more present existence.

You'll notice a sad fact. Most people are *not* free. People constantly think worried thoughts and carry anxiety with them. People *literally* worry themselves sick, whereas your newfound understanding of the inside-out human emotional operating system means you can *unworry* yourself well.

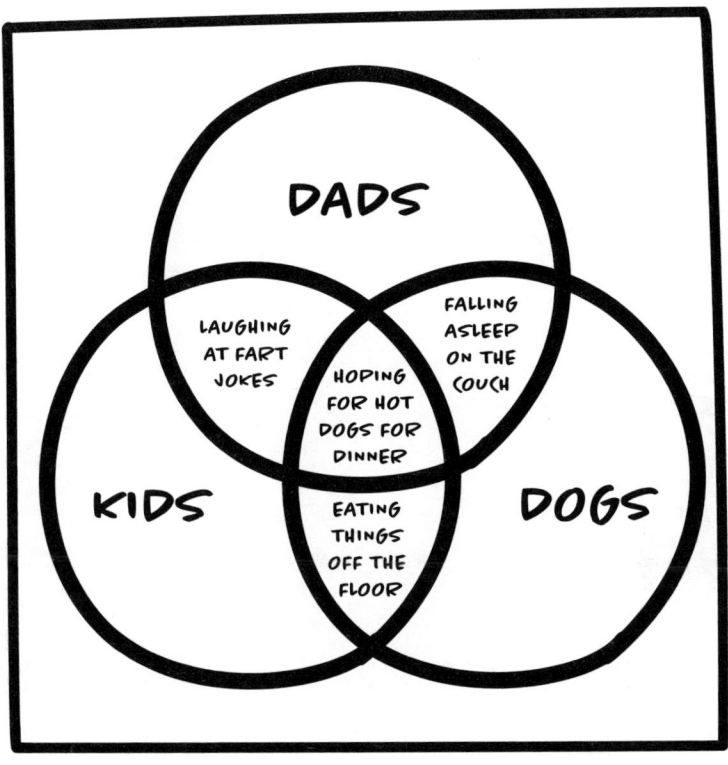

Chapter 10

101 SALVATIONS

DO STUFF. HAVE ADVENTURES. GO PLACES. BE SILLY. NOBODY WANTS TO TALK TO OLD PEOPLE WITH NO STORIES TO TELL!

There's a saying that knowledge is knowing that a tomato is a fruit, and wisdom is not putting it in a fruit salad.

We can't help thinking that most people have plenty of knowledge. We know what we *should* be doing. This section gives you the wisdom part.

LAD FACT

Bananas are berries, but strawberries aren't. In botanical terms, bananas meet the criteria for berries, but strawberries don't.

Here are 101 wonderful pieces of advice that will make you wise beyond your years:

1. You achieve much more by being consistently reliable than by being occasionally amazing.
2. When in doubt, begin.
3. If you want to succeed, double your failure rate.
4. If you swim with a friend, your chances of getting eaten by a shark will drop by 50%.
5. You can't give your life more time but you can give your time more life.
6. Don't let other people ruin your happiness just because they can't find theirs.
7. Your wildest dreams *are* possible.
8. Judging someone doesn't define who they are, it defines who *you* are.
9. The Pratfall effect means that people deem you more attractive if you mess up. Good news, mistakes are sexy!
10. Time heals almost everything. Give time time.
11. It's okay to pee in a wetsuit but inadvisable to fart in a spacesuit.
12. If you want to earn more, learn more.

13. Potatoes wrapped in tin foil and kept in a cupboard become a welcome consolation if your house burns down.
14. Quit trying to be perfect and start being remarkable.
15. We never really grow up; we only learn how to act in public.
16. You're never too old to learn something stupid.
17. There's a huge difference between 'wellbeing' and being 'well off'. Money is nice to have but too many adults chase success so hard that it harms their relationships and wellbeing. If it costs you your mental health, it's too expensive.
18. Being in love can cause shortness of breath and palpitations. The same symptoms as carbon monoxide poisoning.
19. Somewhere between the ages of 17 and 25, travel. Travel light but far, preferably to places where the culture and language are different. You'll come back a better human.
20. Most people know what to do to achieve success. The secrets are simple, but they are not easy. Too many people want, expect or like easy. Hence they never achieve 'success'.
21. Crushes make you stupid. Suddenly, you forget how to form sentences, walk properly or even hold a pencil.
22. Dick pics? Generally not a great idea. Even if it's big and you're proud of it, don't send her a picture of your penis. *Ever!* It's called cyber-flashing. It's sexual harassment and it's illegal.
23. The first time you shave is a disaster. You'll either miss a patch or come out looking like you fought a cheese grater.
24. Group projects are the worst. There's always one person who doesn't do anything and one person who does everything (hint: don't be either).
25. The internet is forever. Past posts will come back to haunt you.
26. Whether it's in school, sports or relationships, hard work beats talent when talent doesn't try. Advice: Give it your best shot, you'll surprise yourself.
27. Be yourself and have a good time; just don't have such a good time that the police are called to the scene. Keep in mind, one really stupid mistake can unravel years of good deeds.

28. Confidence is quiet, not loud. It's not about bragging or being the loudest in the room. Confidence is about being comfortable with yourself, flaws and all.
29. You'll survive heartbreak. That crush who doesn't like you back? It feels huge now, but it won't matter forever.
30. Nobody notices your pimples as much as you do. You're not the only one dealing with acne. Advice: Wash your face, use moisturiser, drink lots of H_2O and stop stressing – it's a phase.
31. Your teachers are real people. Yes, they go home, eat dinner and watch Netflix like everyone else. Treat them with respect. It makes life easier for them and you.
32. Your brain was in full bloom at two. You peaked early, before you could control your bowels. At 14, you *think* you know everything. Much more than your parents, for sure. At 30, you do know some stuff. At 50, you know a lot of stuff. At 90, you know everything but you can't remember any of it. Not even who you are. And your bowels have learned to be two again.
33. Everyone seems normal until you get to know them.
34. Living well really is the best revenge. Being miserable because of a bad or former relationship just might mean that the other person was right about you.
35. A closed mouth gathers no feet.
36. Those who complain the most tend to accomplish the least.
37. Having a plan, even a flawed one at first, is better than no plan at all.
38. What you do every day matters more than what you do every once in a while.
39. The most important person you ever talk to is the one in the mirror.
40. Too many wonderful humans are sleepwalking through their precious days in a digital slumber.
41. Work hard on the days where you have all the drive in the world. And rest more on the days that you don't.
42. Remember that you'll never feel good eating bad food.
43. Exercise, because zombies will eat the slow ones first.
44. Never trust a dog to watch your sandwich.

45. Doing something and getting it wrong is at least ten times more productive than doing nothing.
46. Kindness and hard work together will always carry you farther than intelligence.
47. Being busy and being productive are two different things.
48. When you're up, your friends know who you are. When you're down, you know who your friends are.
49. 'i' before 'e' except after 'Old MacDonald had a farm.'
50. If you're not feeling scared a lot you're probably not doing very much.
51. The world is changed by your example, not your opinion.
52. It hurts to let go but sometimes it's even more painful to hang on.
53. Goals are important. But most people fail because they fail to set behaviours.
54. You can sit in life and wait, and wait, and wait for everything to be perfect. Chances are, you'll die waiting.
55. It doesn't matter what others are doing. It matters what *you* are doing.
56. The greatest mistake you can make in life is to continually be afraid you will make one.
57. Dreams, unlike eggs, don't hatch just by sitting on them.
58. Being nice to someone you dislike doesn't mean you're fake. It means you're mature enough to control your emotions.
59. When you stop chasing the wrong things, you give the right things a chance to catch you.
60. Trying to be somebody you're not is a sure path to self-hate and a waste of the person you are.
61. Giving up doesn't always mean you're weak; sometimes it means you are strong enough and smart enough to let go.
62. Not getting what you want is sometimes a wonderful stroke of luck.
63. A harsh fact of life: bad things do happen to good people. To rub salt into your wounds, good things happen to bad people.
64. No matter how nice the hand soap smells, don't leave the bathroom smelling your fingers.

65. No matter how many mistakes you make or how slow you progress, you are still way ahead of everyone who isn't trying.

66. Things turn out best for people who make the best out of the way things turn out.

67. People are made up of 70% water, and like any other body of water, we feel a deep urge to make our way to the seaside.

68. Money can't buy you happiness, but it can make you really comfortable while you're being miserable.

69. Nobody gets it right every time. We all make bad decisions. We all do stupid things. Just because you mess up doesn't mean you *are* messed up.

70. You will get sucked up by peer pressure and do something stupid. The trick is to not do it too often!

71. Most men have no idea what colour 'mauve' is.

72. You're happiest while you're making the greatest contribution.

73. You miss 100% of the shots you never take.

74. Remember, you're a winner! Out of all those millions of sperm, you got there first. *Rejoice!*

75. Don't be frustrated; be fascinated.

76. Get up early and, while the world sleeps, get busy working on your secret long-term projects.

77. Minor skin grafts can be performed on pigs by covering any cuts and grazes with thin strips of bacon. At least in theory.

78. No great life was ever built on a foundation of excuses.

79. To avoid criticism, do nothing, say nothing and be nothing.

80. People who live in comfort zones are very uncomfortable.

81. Always remember that you are absolutely unique. Just like everyone else.

82. There's no better feeling in the world than a warm pizza box on your lap.

83. Don't spend your life trying to get noticed. Instead, spend it bettering yourself. Then people will notice.

84. Don't believe everything you think.

85. If you find a toilet in your dream, don't use it.

86. The difference between 'try' and 'triumph' is just a little 'umph'.

87. Live life well, not fast.
88. Never eat yellow snow.
89. Control the controllables. Let the rest go.
90. Negative thoughts are like unwanted relatives. If you don't feed them, they soon leave.
91. Be teachable.
92. Nobody thinks they're stupid. That's part of the stupidity.
93. Artificial Intelligence is no match for Natural Stupidity.
94. Give your houseplants names and job titles. Tell visitors, 'This is Samantha, our head of photosynthesis.'
95. When the going gets tough, the weak take a coffee break.
96. He who dies with the most money is nonetheless dead.
97. When your Wi-Fi goes down. Don't panic. Look around and interact with reality.
98. Feelings aren't facts. Feelings are feedback about the content of what we're thinking.
99. Behaviour isn't the problem. Behaviour tells you there is a problem.
100. Trust dogs. They always know whom to stay away from.
101. Next time your mum shouts at you, drape a towel over her shoulders (like a cape) and say, 'Now you're Super Angry'. Might work. Might not.

Chapter 11

LEVEL UP

Chapter Summary

This is a cracking chapter aimed at boys who are seeking next level achievements. The genuinely committed. The lads who have a passion to make it in something, to be someone, to rise to the top in sport, the arts, science, comedy, rock stardom, YouTubing (or whatever).

This content isn't for everyone. If you're okay being middle of the pack, comfortable with regrets and content with operating well within your capabilities, look away now. There's always a video buffering or a game to be played.

But we figure that if you've come this far, you're up for some bonus content that'll set you up for life. This section takes the learning from posh watches, points you to WOOP goals and guides you towards action, not distraction. Then there's a double helping of the ef-word, a section on how to get results rather than excuses, before we strongly encourage you to be a quitter.

You'll want to stick around for the chapter finale which contains the powerful truth about how to multiply your earnings 100 times over.

Grab a highlighter pen. You'll be wanting to remind yourself of the stand out paragraphs. Pair up, in threes, and away we go . . .

Marginal gains

Yogi Berra is a famous American baseball player who's better known for what he said than what he did. Here are some of his quotes that have gone down in legend as 'Yogi-isms': *'You can observe a lot by just watching'* is genius. You have to think about *'No one goes there nowadays, it's too crowded'* before its ridiculousness hits you. He once took a training session and asked everyone to *'Pair up in threes.'*

Having softened you up with some genuine Yogi-isms, here's something that sounds like one, but isn't: *When you're in the top 10%, you're only 50% there.*

Eh?

It's relatively easy to be in the top 10% of anything. Show up, apply yourself, work hard consistently, and you'll fly. The key word is *consistently*. You'll take giant strides forward simply because most people are coasting, and you're not. They might have the skills, but not the application.

In cycling they call it the peloton – the chasing pack (French for platoon). The reason most riders don't want to lead the race is because there are advantages of being in the peloton. It's the same with life. Leading from the front requires a load of the dreaded ef-word: *effort*. It's a whole lot easier, safer and more comfortable to be part of the chasing pack.[168]

How much of the ef-word you choose to use is entirely up to you. It's your call. This section isn't about that; it's about our confusing sentence from two paragraphs ago: *when you're in the top 10%, you're only 50% there.*

Let's unpick it, using a Premier League football academy as an example. Here's the scenario – you're a decent footballer with lots of natural talent which, if you combine with the ef-word, gets you into the school team. With a bit more of the ef-word, you become the best player and captain of said team. Your team beats their bitter rivals in an epic inter-school cup final, you score a superb solo goal, and a Premier League scout invites you for a trial.

Squeaky bum time. You've landed yourself a massive opportunity with fame, fortune and a Nike contract just a sniff away. All you have to do is impress, which is of course what you've been doing for the past ten years. You've worked hard to get into the top 10%, but you're only 50% of the way there.

Why?

Because everyone at the academy is in the top 10%. They're all captains of their school teams who also score terrific solo goals, so you're no longer pack leader, you're *in* the pack. At this level, you're bang average. You've worked your socks off to get into the top 10%, but the academy only signs players who are in the top 1%.

That's why getting into the top 10% is the halfway mark. Becoming elite is the next 50%.

You look around at the other players and they're all amazing. All that extra effort that's taken you to the top means you get to keep pace, but you stop rising. Getting into the top 1% is a different ball game. So how do you accelerate again?

First up, you have to keep on doing the good habits that got you into the 10%, but there's more because what gets you into the top 1% isn't necessarily the same as what got you into the top 10%.

Back to cycling. A while back the British cycling team coined the phrase 'marginal gains' that elevated them from perennial under-performers to multiple gold medal winners. To be clear, their goals remained the same. The British cycling team always set out to win gold, but the team now refocused on processes. It was a case of re-examining everything to see if they could go faster. Tiny details mattered. A tenth of a second here, a hundredth there . . . in a sport where winner and second place was often down to hundredths of a second, these tiny details mattered.

Some of it sounds sensible and logical. For example, British cycling used a wind tunnel to eke out small improvements to aerodynamics. Cue newly designed bikes, kit and helmets (= 3% improvement). But other changes sound a bit weird. They hired a surgeon to teach the athletes about proper hand-washing so as to avoid illnesses during competition (0.5%) and they also decided not to shake any hands during the Olympics (0.5%). They brought their own mattresses and pillows so the athletes could sleep in the same posture every night (0.7%).

They searched everywhere for marginal gains and, added together, they added up to gold.

GB rowing applied the same principle but in their case it was a consistent question, 'Will it make the boat go faster?', which triggered a series of 1% improvements that were worth their weight in gold.

> 7 words that will change your life:
>
> Do it better than you have to

But the lessons spill way beyond sport. This is our elite chapter. We put a warning upfront, it's not for everyone. But your eyeballs have reached this far, so you're interested in metaphorically *making your boat go faster* which in your case is *making your future life better*.

This could be a whole range of things that move you from the top 10% to the top 1%. Accelerating your natural ability in a subject area. Getting a place at a *top* university. Smoothing the pathway to a stellar career. Becoming an elite cricketer. Getting extraordinary exam results. Making a career out of art/music/dance . . .

Linking back to the Life Maxx matrix (reprinted below because we know you've forgotten), it's about engaging in *more* of the game-changer activities *more* of the time. If you're serious about committing to doing important tasks that require effort, you need to prepare yourself for repetition and boredom because here's a surprising truth. If you look at the *elite*, the top 0.1% of any sport or occupation (the ones who are absolutely smashing it), they have been willing to suffer and struggle.

Bluntly, everyone wants to have an epic life but not very many can be truly bothered to graft for it.

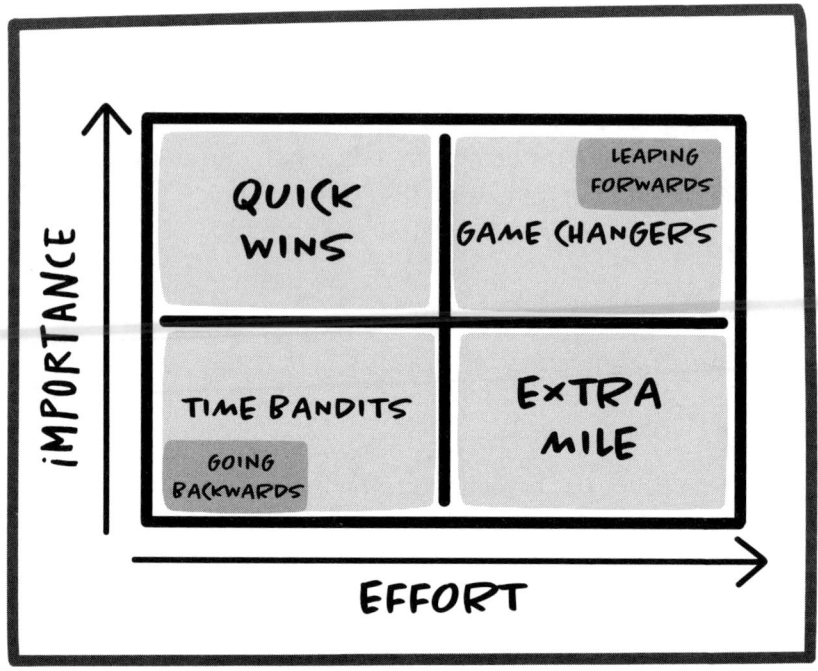

WOOP

I saw an advertisement for a posh watch. It's the kind of timepiece that costs more than your average family car. The ad consists of an impossibly good looking bloke teaching his improbably good looking son to sail a yacht. Chances are that when the impossibly good looking man eventually passes away, the improbably good looking son will finally get to wear the watch. The ad comes with a cheesy strapline about never actually owning the watch, just keeping it for the next generation.

Anyhow, one of the selling points is that this particular timepiece is water resistant to 400 metres. So I googled it. For info, if you go snorkelling, your head implodes at 15 metres. If you are a trained diver and enter the ocean with all the SCUBA gear, you should be okay to about 50 metres. The deepest 'free dive' on record (meaning a dive done without any gear) was 253 metres. Upon surfacing, the man who achieved this new world record immediately had a stroke.[169]

There's good news and bad news about waggling your flippers down to 400 metres. Bad news: your body will implode, your eyeballs will pop and your skull will be crushed to the size of a golf ball. Good news: your watch will still be working and presumably, once your body is hauled from the depths, it'll be ripped off your wrist and passed on to the next generation.

Ridiculousness aside, it brings me to a different kind of over-engineering, and to an innocent question: are we over-engineering our goals?

You might have heard of well-meaning but misguided SMART goals. If not, *phew!* Well done on avoiding them. Almost every school and business uses them, but just because everyone else is taught to set SMART goals doesn't mean they're the right thing to do. SMART goals are a waste of time unless you want to commit to living way below your potential. I'm not going to trot out the whole acronym but 'R' stands for 'realistic' and 'A' is for 'achievable'. Seriously? If you only ever commit to what's realistic and achievable you'll end up mopping floors somewhere.

If you're heading into elite territory, you need to max out and dream big, in which case WOOP will fit the bill. WOOP stands for Whopper, Outcome, Obstacle, Plan, and is super useful if you're intent on turning big dreams into reality.

W is about setting a WHOPPER of a goal. What do you want to accomplish? An ambition. A dream. Not something that can be achieved by tomorrow or next week. It might be two years away, or seven, or 15. The thing about your WHOPPER is that it has to be exciting. Something challenging. The W needs to be on the outer edges of your achievability.

O is for OUTCOME. Using your best imagination, the O requires you to picture your WHOPPER of a goal. Maybe run it as a movie in your head. It's the director's cut, so you can turn up the colours and feelings. Play your bright future in wide-screen, surround-sound, technicolour WOW-mode.

It's a WHOPPER, and the OUTCOME is truly exciting, but the second O asks you to anticipate the OBSTACLES. What might get in the way of you achieving your goal? There are always things that will trip you up. It could be lack of focus, a belief, doom scrolling, a mild case of *can't-be-botheredness* or a bad habit. For example, it's easy to be distracted by a games console. It's easy to skip training because it's raining. The key to anticipating the OBSTACLES is that if you know they're coming, they are less likely to trip you up, which leads to . . .

P = PLAN. It helps if you plan for the obstacles to happen *before* they happen, and to make promises to yourself. So, if _____ [obstacle happens], then I will _____ [action you promise to take].

Common obstacles are fear of failure, laziness, lack of focus, lack of motivation, distractions, making excuses, negative thoughts and lack of confidence.

So your actions could be any or all of: take a breath, go for it, act confident, be determined, seek help, think about something similar that I have achieved . . .

Here's a personal WOOP example that helped me write this book.

My WHOPPER of a goal was to write a book that would give teenage boys a leg up to an amazing life.

The movie in my head had an epic OUTCOME with me seeing *LADULT* in the bookshops and getting invited to do talks in schools.

The OBSTACLES were mostly negative self-talk and work pressures. Both Ollie and I work full time, so we were going to have to magic extra hours from somewhere.

My PLAN sentence was this: When time pressures kick in (which they will), I will cut Netflix and work into the evenings instead.

And WOOP, a bit of hardship and a few missed Netflix binges and here we are!

You could do a school WOOP, a home WOOP, a skill WOOP, an exam WOOP, a future career WOOP. . . or no WOOP.

But real life's not like Disney. Your fairytale happy ending tends not to happen by accident. Your 'happy ever after' is more likely to come true if you have a clear vision and a plan. WOOP delivers both.

Click 'Refresh'

Kokorozashi (Japanese): Where the heart points

Imagine a personal mission, a passion that occupies your thoughts on the weekend and makes you excited to wake up on Monday morning. Would you be willing to commit years, possibly decades, to this cause? If so, then you may have found your *kokorozashi*.

Note, most people never find their *kokorozashi*. They drift. It can be interpreted as will, motivation, ambition, a sense of purpose, or personal mission. *Kokorozashi* brings clarity to your heart and mind and enriches your life.

Action not distraction

It's great fun to plan your WOOP goal, but the magic ingredient is ACTION!

For example, your WOOP is to run a marathon. You've bought the Lycra and the running shoes. What happens next? Nothing! Nothing, that is, until you take *action*.

Your WOOP goal is to get your eating habits into shape. You've persuaded your parents to stack the fridge full of fruit and veg. What happens next? Nothing! Nothing, that is, until you take *action*.

Your WOOP goal is to smash your exams. You've spent three hours creating your whizz bang colour-coded revision timetable. You've posted it on your bedroom wall. What happens next? Nothing! Nothing, that is, until you take *action*.

Your WOOP goal is to find a girlfriend. You've sat and looked at the amazing human being. You've caught her eye a couple of times. You've dreamt of chatting to her. There she is, sitting there, scrolling on her phone. What happens next? Nothing! Nothing, that is, until you take *action*.

This is where most people go wrong. They spend most of their time wishing that their WOOP dream will come true because, let's face it, visualising how amazing your life is going to be when you've achieved your goal is the easy part. You can create all sorts of fancy planners, to-do lists, all colour coded with neat labels and stickers on them. You can do just a bit more research. But sooner or later you've got to actually get off your backside and take some ACTION.

Oh, and one more thing about WOOP goals. The whole point of them is that they're massive. Sometimes people give up way too early on their huge ambition because of how hard it is and how little reward they seem to be getting for the effort they're putting in. You go to the gym twice and you've got sore biceps but no noticeable difference in muscle mass. You rock up at football training for two whole weeks and you're still on the subs' bench. You eat a healthy lunch Monday through to Friday but you can still pinch an inch. You've cut this week's screen time by 30% and are still not top of the class.

That's because there's a lag between creating a great habit and seeing a noticeable difference (with the exception of sleep. Get good quality sleep and you'll notice improvements in energy and concentration straight away).

So our advice is to be aware of the lag between action and improvement. Most habits have a tipping point where, all of a sudden, something extra kicks in. You'll know when you reach it because things get noticeably easier, and all the extra effort makes sense. Once the habit is grooved in, it's easier to keep going than to stop.

Our final word on goal setting is a reminder. In previous chapters we've spoken about living in a world of distraction. It's easy to get sidetracked by something new, shiny and interesting. In the modern world, your ability to stay focused is quite a thing. It's more of an ability than ever before.

The 60/90 rule

If you want to achieve a BIG goal, get up an hour early, dedicate the first 60 minutes of your day to it for the next 90 days. No distractions. No interruptions. No excuses.

The Greek word *euthymia* is the sense of our own path and how to stay on it without getting distracted by all the others that intersect it. In other words, it's not about beating or bettering anyone else. It's not about having more than the others. It's about staying focused on your WOOP goal without succumbing to all the things that draw you away from it.[170]

That's euthymia.

Maybe your priority is exams. Or maybe it's family. Maybe it's influence or fame. Maybe it's building a business, or being a surgeon/soldier/nurse/teacher/builder/etc. All of these are perfectly fine motivations. But beware, there will be a million distractions pulling you away.

Oh, and one more thing about BIG goals. You don't have to know exactly how you'll get there. But you do have to start, often before you think you're ready.

The ef-word

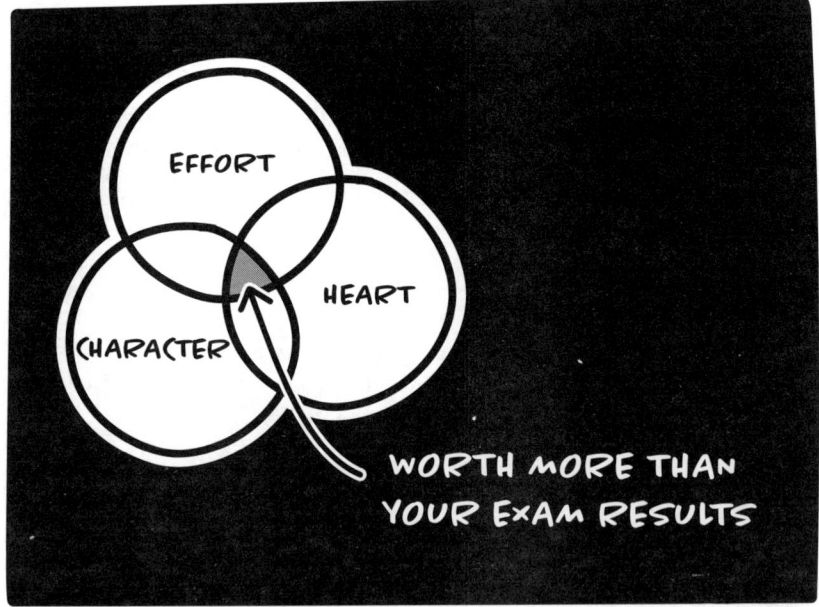

Teachers talk about 'growth mindsets' all the time, but please allow us to remind you of the basics. Fixed and growth mindset language came into being as a result of some research done by Carol Dweck.

Long story short, Carol worked with hundreds of 11-year-olds and in phase one, she set a series of puzzles and then gave them their feedback. Half were given praise which suggested they were gifted and talented (she used phrases along the lines of 'you are so smart at this') and the others were given praise that reflected the effort they'd put in (for example, 'you must have worked really hard').

Phase two sounds like an experiment in child cruelty. Carol gave the kids another test – a much harder one – in fact so tough it was impossible. Of course, none of the kids did very well, but she discovered that those who'd been given praise for their intelligence soon gave up, whereas those praised for effort persevered and, against the odds, improved their scores by 30%.[171]

Which is kind of interesting, but so what?

If we mash up the growth mindset research with that of Professor Angela Duckworth,[172] things really hot up. Keeping it simple, if you want to become *skilful* at something it helps if you have a bit of natural talent. But talent isn't usually enough because:

Skill = Talent × Effort

Talent relates to how fast we can improve in skill. Using tennis as an example, a little bit of talent is useful, but talent without effort means you'll never get skilful.

That's part one. Once you've got skilful, ask yourself what makes the breakthrough to world-class achievement?

Achievement = Skill × Effort

You'll notice that effort figures again. In Angela Duckworth's research, effort counts *twice*. You won't acquire skill without it, and you won't achieve without putting effort into honing your skills. Basically, hard work beats talent when talent doesn't work hard.

Sure, natural talent might give you a head-start, but it's no guarantee that you'll stay ahead. In fact, relying on natural talent alone leads to complacency, and one day you wake up average. It's hard work that makes the dream work.

Delving (yet again) into deep stuff that most books don't tell you, at the core of all human behaviour, most people's needs are more or less similar. We want positive experiences because they make us feel great. It's negative experiences that we all struggle with, but to be a high achiever you are going to put yourself through the mill. For example, you might want to do really well in your exams but that means working hard in class, plus long hours of study in your own time.

Counter-intuitively, the question may be less about what you want to achieve and more like, 'What pain are you willing to sustain to achieve it?' So in the interests of challenging you, it's worth pondering what your WOOP goals might be, and what pain and sacrifices you're willing to go through to achieve them.

Click 'Refresh'

Before the biggest game of their season, the coach of Tampa Bay Buccaneers had a huge granite rock deposited in the locker room and a poster on the wall that read:

When nothing seems to help, I go look at a stonecutter hammering away at his rock, perhaps a hundred times without as much as a crack showing in it. Yet at the hundred and first blow it will split in two, and I know it was not that blow that did it, but all that had gone before.

The coach used this – the stonecutter's creed – as a reminder that the rock doesn't split the first time. It takes thousands of blows with a hammer and chisel to make something happen. Creating repeatable habits is more likely to lead to success. This is especially true for routine every day, pounding-the-rock-type tasks like exercising, revising, learning, guitar practice . . .

The stonecutter's creed also reminds us that it's not really appropriate to give credit to the last blow for cracking the rock. For example, the glory tends to go to the person who scores the decisive penalty in a shootout, or the keeper who makes the save. Metaphorically, that's the last blow that split the rock, but let's not forget the other players' efforts in landing blow after blow to get to the point of cracking the rock.

Quit trying

Counter-intuitively, to join the elite you have to be a quitter. Quit mindless screen time, quit blaming, quit winning petty battles, quit coasting, quit bad food, quit low-level grumbling, quit anything that's hampering your progress.

The message is clear: *stop putting effort into what's stopping you*.

But most of all, to be in the elite, you need to quit trying. Unless used in a rugby context, the word 'try' is a shocker. It takes you backwards. Every time you announce (quietly to yourself, or audibly to those around you), 'I'm going to *try* to . . . get fit, be there, show up, eat healthy, get amazing grades, work hard, behave better, get more sleep,' you're setting yourself up to fail. Lose the word 'try', and the sentences come alive with intent: 'I'm going to . . . get fit, be there, show up, eat healthy, get amazing grades, work hard, behave better, get more sleep.'

Losing 'try' from your vocab moves you from excuses to results.

AWARDS YOU DON'T WANT TO WIN...

'PRETENDING YOU'RE OKAY WHEN YOU'RE NOT' MARTYR AWARD

MOST SCREEN HOURS

'NEVER ASKING FOR HELP' TROPHY

'BOTTLING IT ALL UP INSIDE' GOLD STAR

'COUNTING DOWN TO THE WEEKEND' LIFETIME ACHIEVEMENT

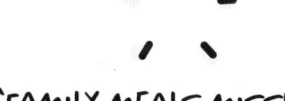

'FAMILY MEALS MISSED' ABSENCE MEDAL

'HOURS PROCRASTINATED' GENIUS LEVEL

THE OMG-AWARD FOR 'MOST MILES SCROLLED'

Do you want results or excuses?

A lesson from adult-land is that too many people demand change but don't want *to* change. They talk a good talk. They know exactly what they need to do, but they're not doing it!

As a rule, I have more people tell me why they can't change than why they can. And while I acknowledge that we all have challenges, hurdles and obstacles to navigate, and most reasons are, in fact, not reasons at all.

They are *excuses*.

Let's explain, so the penny drops while you're still young enough for it to make a massive difference.

You can get lulled into making excuse after excuse after excuse after excuse . . . *after excuse*. Until you start to slide into mediocrity. Develop a habit of excuses and you'll develop a stench of decay.

So here's a fact . . . there's a huge difference between a reason and an excuse.

On the surface, reasons and excuses share a similar strand of DNA. The principal difference lies in the results of each. It's all about the actions that follow. A reason explains something. It's an acknowledgement of fault which you then take responsibility for, and action follows. An excuse justifies, blames or defends a fault, with the intent to shift responsibility. It's not fair, or it's someone else's fault, or it's too difficult. When you trot out an excuse, it lets you off the hook. Your sins are excused.

If you're still struggling with the difference between a reason and an excuse, here's an excellent rule of thumb – every *reason* must have a resulting *action*. That's so important we'll sharpen it with an extra word . . . every reason must have a resulting *positive* action.

Reason implies that fault is recognised and accepted, and that you step up and take accountability for your actions. Whereas an excuse exists to justify, blame or defend a fault, with the intent to wriggle out of taking responsibility.

An excuse will NEVER be followed by positive, goal-directed or solution-oriented behaviour. Excuses bring productivity to a screeching halt. They waste time and murder potential. Do not associate with them. Ever.

'My teacher's always picking on me.' That can be a neat excuse for why you don't like going to that class, or it can be a reason to change. Once you flip it into a reason, the action might be: *'So I'm going to knuckle down and work so hard that they'll be singling me out for praise instead.'*

'It was a really difficult exam paper' is a superb excuse for not doing very well. All of a sudden, fluffing the exam isn't your fault, it's the examiner's fault. Flip it into a reason and it's followed up with, *'So I need to work extra hard to make sure I don't get tripped up again.'*

'I overslept,' 'I'm too tired,' 'I'm not a morning person,' 'I've got too much homework,' 'It's too difficult' – these are classic excuses for almost every situation.

Warning: excuses pose a clear and present danger to your future. Delete them, swap them for reasons, and BE THE CHANGE.

WORK HARD, FEEL GOOD.
FEEL GOOD, PERFORM GOOD.
PERFORM GOOD, EARN GOOD!

How to multiply your earnings

Here's something else that nobody ever tells you . . . there's something that adds even more value to the already heady heights of 'elite'.

It just so happens that emotions are contagious. It's obvious when you think about it, but most people don't. When my football team wins, 30,000 people skip away, happy as can be. When we lose, there's a mass contagion of negativity and a chorus of 'sack the manager'.

But contagion also happens on a much smaller scale. We're sending out messages to our fellow human beings. Our state affects their state. We cannot say it any simpler than this – the way you feel affects how those around you feel.

That means there are tremendous side effects to feeling amazing. Sure, you'll find that you start having (a) an effortlessly clear mind, (b) more time for what's important, (c) improved decision-making, (d) better performance where it counts and (e) more of the results that matter to you.

But so will those around you!

In the adult world, it's called 'leadership', and it's one of the most sought after things in the business and sporting worlds. If you can bring leadership, you can multiply your earnings 10 times over. Maybe 20. Possibly 100.

Because being the best IN the team is one thing, but being the best FOR the team is leadership. By 'team' we mean being the best *for* the classroom, friendship group, family, neighbourhood, sports team, after school club etc. Bringing your best self to the situation helps other people to raise their game. Once you start bringing the best out in other people, that's a total game-changer because that's how to create a winning team.

Hey, you're young, and we don't want to add any pressure. The previous paragraph comes into play when you're a bit older. You'll go on lots of courses that will train you to be a leader, but in terms of keeping it simple, honest and real, you already are a leader. People will catch how you feel. Those in your classroom, family and team have no choice but to catch how you feel (because that's how humans are designed).

The 10-million-dollar question you need to ask yourself is this: *what are they catching?*

Chapter 12

TOWARDS A NEW DEFINITION OF MASCULINITY

Chapter Summary

Thanks for being with us on the *LADULT* journey. This final section ties up some loose ends and gives you one last nudge into 'best self' territory. It's a reminder that you're like a yoghurt – you have a best-before date.

You've got plenty of time before you curdle, so live it FULLY. Have more picnics and more 'moments'. Your job is to shine brightly in an imperfect world.

Our advice is to live your life as though everything you do will be documented by the internet and available to see by anyone for all eternity. There's a high probability your great-great-grandchildren will study your life for a homework assignment, so be sure you make them proud of what they see.

This chapter will help make that happen. But first, here's some breakfast thinking.

Snap, crackle and pop

Here's a lovely thought from author, motivational speaker and all-round good guy Gavin Oattes.

Imagine coming downstairs for breakfast and pouring yourself a big bowl of Rice Krispies. Keep imagining, as it sits there before you, in all its dry, boring, bland beigeness. Add a sprinkle of sugar and what happens?

Absolutely nothing, that's what!

But add a glug of milk and it's party time! There's a whole lot of snap, crackle and popping as those critters start to shake their little Rice Krispie asses. If you don't start eating, they'll twerk themselves right out of the bowl.

They turn from inert to jumpin', from boring to exciting, from lifeless to party animal, at a drop of the white stuff.

Gav's point?

That bowl is like your life!

You can sit and look at life forever. You can hope, dream, jump up and down and shout at life. You can worry about the blandness. You can compare your Rice Krispies with everyone else's Rice Krispies. You can add extra sugar!

Or you can *be the milk!*

YOU are the vital ingredient that makes life snap, crackle and pop.

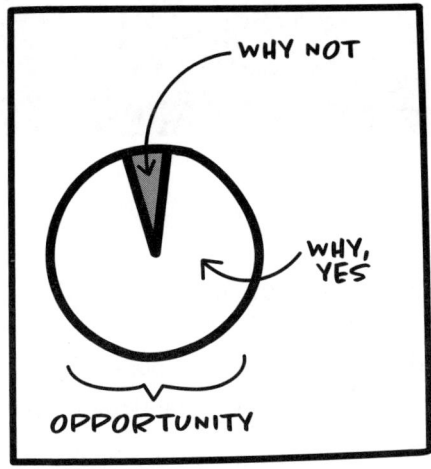

The sad fact is that too many people live their life as a bowl of *dry* Rice Krispies. They forget that they're the secret ingredient and end up living a *woulda, coulda, shoulda* existence. Adventures not adventured. Experiences not experienced. Boundaries not pushed. Countries not visited. Grudges carried forward. Belly laughs unlaughed. Rollercoasters not roller-coasted. Loved ones taken for granted. Dances not danced. Sunrises unseen. Calculated risks not taken. Depths not plunged. Moments unnoticed. Waves un-surfed. Hugs un-hugged. Potential un-explored. Stars un-gazed. Puddles un-jumped. Picnics un-picnicked. Snowmen un-built.

Ultimately, these missed opportunities lead to the scariest thing of all – *a life un-lived*.

The caped crusader

Congratulations! You've made it to the end of *LADULT*. Your eyeballs have scanned left to right across 50,000 words! Some will have sunk in, and some forgotten, which is why we're looping back to the question that kick-started chapter one: in the swirling mass of confusion, *what is a real man?*

LADULT has been big on role-modelling what the world needs, which is of course you at your absolute best. The you who adds value to the world. The you who simultaneously navigates relationships with your laddish mates while also being someone who makes girls feel safe, respected and heard.

This hints at a much bigger point. Not all men are able to walk that line. It's accepting that although you're not to blame for how some other men behave, you do have the power to create positive change by role-modelling what's right.

To help you ease into this new type of man, we're going to finish by breaking our new definition down into four sections: Confidence, Attitude, Presence and Enthusiasm. The CAPE model will elevate you to everyday superhero status by enhancing your abilities. Things like viz-ABILITY, like-ABILITY, adapt-ABILITY, response-ABILITY and account-ABILITY are day-to-day qualities that will make people go 'WOW!'

Let's break CAPE down . . .

Confidence

A genuine sense of self-confidence is a great place to start. Reminder: true confidence doesn't require you to be the loudest in the room or always be the centre of attention, and it certainly doesn't require you to be constantly proving yourself to others. We're talking about *real* confidence, which is quiet but noticeable.

True confidence is earned by proving to yourself, again and again, that you are capable of the things you set your sights on, and that you can wake up each day knowing you'll be at your best. It's the confidence to admit when you make a mistake, and to take the lessons from it to be better next time around. True confidence means that you know that your mistakes do not define you, nor make you a failure. It's knowing that the world might not always be fair, but that doesn't mean that it is against you. Instead of letting the world force you into submission, you take the challenges head on.

Honestly, lack of confidence is mildly unattractive and over-confidence is hideously ugly. *Genuine* self-confidence is the sexiest thing you'll ever wear. It brings a smile to your face and puts a spring in your step. But it's even bigger than that. True confidence is reassuring for those around you. Your security and assuredness will draw in friends and relationships purely by virtue of you being confidently you.

Attitude

Nothing sums up the 'A' for 'Attitude' better than our seven-word phrase from the middle of the book: *Do it better than you have to.*

Out of everything in your life, your attitude is the smallest thing that makes the biggest difference. It's like a muscle. The more you exercise your positive attitude, the stronger it gets.

Every single day, without fail, you will be presented with situations where your attitude will dictate your actions. Homework, exams, relationships, breakups, *big* life decisions – the attitude you choose to adopt will influence the outcome in each situation. If you can consciously *choose* a positive attitude, an attitude of *do it better than you have to*, you'll find that more often than not the results speak for themselves. Not everything will always go your way, but when that happens your attitude will dictate how you respond (give up, go again, change your approach or learn something).

The great men, and indeed women, of history would not be remembered today if they accepted defeat at the first hurdle. Craft an attitude that works for you rather than against you, and once again, people will go 'WOW!'

Presence

Real men are powerful people not because they boss people around or dominate others by force, but because they have *presence*. It's much more than just being there; it boils down to this: if you're going to be in the room, BE in the room.

Fully!

Be interested in other people. Make eye contact. Ask questions. Get off your screen and into people's real lives.

Presence is an everyday superpower simply because of its rarity value. Everyone else is distracted – *absent* in their presence – busy missing the opportunity for genuine human connection. Presence is an everyday superpower because it creates a connection. It's an olive branch to relationships, a wormhole into the present moment and a hook-up with your best self.

Presence requires power over yourself. The screens are calling you. Your brain will always be tempted to veer off course. Mastery over yourself means you have the power to say no to the little pleasure goblin inside your head until you've really *earned it*; it's the power to think about the long term rather than caving in for that short-term hit, whatever it is.

The power of presence will seep into *every* corner of your life and will put you far ahead of the pack. You'll work harder, you'll exercise on the days you don't feel like it, and you'll know when to enjoy yourself without taking it too far. Your mind and your body will be sharp, giving you the wonderful opportunity to see what you are truly capable of.

Enthusiasm

Finally, and ever so importantly, the E in CAPE is for enthusiasm. We're not talking about enthusiasm just for the things you enjoy or for the things that you excel in. We are talking about enthusiasm for life itself.

Look around at family, teachers and friends and you'll see it's easy to let your enthusiasm halo slip. Why? Because your brain is wired for negativity. It's so easy to focus on all the things that you wish were different and on all the things that you don't have. The miracle of simply being alive can slip your mind.

So don't let it!

Drink from the jug of enthusiasm. Get thirsty. Glug it down. We believe the best men, the best women, the best *anyone*, are the people who are engaged with life itself.

So our final challenge is to wear the CAPE. Live with *CONFIDENCE*, choose a great *ATTITUDE*, be *PRESENT* and engage *ENTHUSIASTICALLY*.

In the Marvel Universe, immortality is seen as the ultimate superpower but in our world, *mortality* is your secret weapon. The fact you've got a best-before date means you've got to get busy living.

The CAPE model hints at the massive difference between 'being alive' and 'truly living'. Being alive involves having a pulse, whereas truly living requires it to race a bit. It makes sense to throw yourself wholeheartedly into life. To shine. In psychology there's a term, 'collective effervescence', which refers to a bunch of people who are shining brightly. So, for example, when one person shines, they light up their family, a team or their classroom.

So what are you waiting for?

LADULT has been about learning how to live full beam ahead because, as far as we're concerned, that fabled light at the end of the tunnel *may as well be you!*

References

1. Reed, M.S., Evely, A.C., Cundill, G. et al. (2010). What is social learning? *Ecology and Society* 15 (4): 1–10.
2. Bunker, C.J. and Varnum, M.E.W. (2021). How strong is the association between social media use and false consensus? *Computers in Human Behavior* 125: 106947.
3. DeCecco, J.P. and Elia, J.P. (1993). A critique and synthesis of biological essentialism and social constructionist views of sexuality and gender. *Journal of Homosexuality* 24 (3–4): 1–26.
4. Chant, S.H. and Gutmann, M.C. (2000). *Mainstreaming Men into Gender and Development: Debates, Reflections, and Experiences.* Oxford: Oxfam.
5. Schopf, J.W. (1978). The evolution of the earliest cells. *Scientific American* 239 (3): 110–139.
6. Goodenough, U. and Heitman, J. (2014). Origins of eukaryotic sexual reproduction. *Cold Spring Harbor Perspectives in Biology* 6 (3): a016154.
7. Mesnick, S. and Ralls, K. (2018). Sexual dimorphism. In: *Encyclopedia of Marine Mammals*, 3rd (ed. B. Würsig, J.G.M. Thewissen, and K.M. Kovacs), 848–853. Burlington: Academic Press.
8. Pietsch, T.W. (1976). Dimorphism, parasitism and sex: reproductive strategies among deepsea ceratioid anglerfishes. *Copeia* 781–793.
9. Birkhead, T.R., Lee, K.E., and Young, P. (1988). Sexual cannibalism in the praying mantis *Hierodula membranacea. Behaviour* 112–118.
10. Lassek, W.D. and Gaulin, S.J. (2022). Substantial but misunderstood human sexual dimorphism results mainly from sexual selection on males and natural selection on females. *Frontiers in Psychology* 13: 859931.
11. Hunter, S.K., Angadi, S.S., Bhargava, A. et al. (2023). The biological basis of sex differences in athletic performance: consensus statement for the American College of Sports Medicine. *Translational Journal of the American College of Sports Medicine* 8 (4): 1–33.
12. Kelly, R.L. (2013). *The Lifeways of Hunter-gatherers: The Foraging Spectrum.* Cambridge: Cambridge University Press.

13. Hackel, H. and Kelly, C. (2008). *Reading Women: Literacy, Authorship, and Culture in the Atlantic World, 1500–1800*. Pennsylvania: University of Pennsylvania Press.
14. Crawford, C. and Greaves, E. (2015, November). Socio-economic, ethnic and gender differences in HE participation. BIS Research Paper No. 18.
15. Ging, D. (2019). Alphas, betas, and incels: theorizing the masculinities of the manosphere. *Men and Masculinities* 22 (4): 638–657.
16. Canbolat, M., Senol, D., Cevirgen, F., and Ozbag, D. (2018). An anatomic overview to "manspreading" campaign. *Annals of Medical Research* 25 (3): 499–502.
17. Giuzio Carvalho Macedo, D. (2023). *What it means to be a man: Measuring the extent between self-reported toxic masculine beliefs and social anxiety levels in college men aged 18 to 25.*
18. Brahmbhatt, M., Canuto, O., and Vostroknutova, E. (2010). Dealing with Dutch disease. 2010. *World Bank - Economic Premise*: 1–7
19. Wortman, J. and Wood, D. (2011). The personality traits of liked people. *Journal of Research in Personality* 45 (6): 519–528.
20. Sutherland, R. (2020). What bees can teach us about efficiency. *The Spectator* (25 April).
21. Haub, C. (1995). How many people have ever lived on earth? *Population Today* 23 (2): 4–5.
22. Rivera, R.M. and Bennett, L.B. (2010). Epigenetics in humans: an overview. *Current Opinion in Endocrinology, Diabetes and Obesity* 17 (6): 493–499.
23. Baldwin, J. (2012). Obesity kills more people than hunger. *Al Jazeera* (14 December).
24. Skulmowski, A. and Xu, K.M. (2022). Understanding cognitive load in digital and online learning: a new perspective on extraneous cognitive load. *Educational Psychology Review* 34 (1): 171–196.
25. Norris, C.J. (2021). The negativity bias, revisited: evidence from neuroscience measures and an individual differences approach. *Social Neuroscience* 16 (1): 68–82.

26. Gordon, E.M., Chauvin, R.J., Van, A.N. et al. (2023). A somato-cognitive action network alternates with effector regions in motor cortex. *Nature* 617 (7960): 351–359.

27. Pace T. The Human Brain in the Modern World. Arcadia. 2022 Sep 19. Available from https://www.byarcadia.org/post/the-human-brain-in-the-modern-world

28. Craske, M.G., Rauch, S.L., Ursano, R. et al. (2011). What is an anxiety disorder? *Focus* 9 (3): 369–388.

29. Hidaka, B.H. (2012). Depression as a disease of modernity: explanations for increasing prevalence. *Journal of Affective Disorders* 140 (3): 205–214.

30. Yasmeen, R., Aslam, I., Ahmad, M., and Shah, M.H.A. (2023). Zoochosis: a short review on stereotypical behavior of captive animals. *Journal of Wildlife and Biodiversity* 7 (2): 8–20.

31. McAllister, S. (2024). What is it like to be neurodivergent? (18 March).

32. Young, S., Adamo, N., Ásgeirsdóttir, B.B. et al. (2020). Females with ADHD: an expert consensus statement taking a lifespan approach providing guidance for the identification and treatment of attention-deficit/hyperactivity disorder in girls and women. *BMC Psychiatry* 20: 1–27.

33. Sherfey, M.J. (1974). Some biology of sexuality. *Journal of Sex & Marital Therapy* 1 (2): 97–109.

34. BBC. When do babies recognise themselves in the mirror? https://www.bbc.co.uk/tiny-happy-people/articles/zdt3vk7 (accessed 01/07/2025).

35. Arain, M., Haque, M., Johal, L. et al. (2013). Maturation of the adolescent brain. *Neuropsychiatric Disease and Treatment* 449–461.

36. França, T.F.A. and Pompeia, S. (2023). Reappraising the role of dopamine in adolescent risk-taking behavior. *Neuroscience & Biobehavioral Reviews* 147: 105085.

37. Schwartz, P.D., Maynard, A.M., and Uzelac, S.M. (2008). Adolescent egocentrism: a contemporary view. *Adolescence* 43 (171): 441–448.

38. Somerville, L.H., Jones, R.M., Ruberry, E.J. et al. (2013). The medial prefrontal cortex and the emergence of self-conscious emotion in adolescence. *Psychological Science* 24 (8): 1554–1562.

39. Gilovich, T., Kruger, J., and Medvec, V.H. (2002). The spotlight effect revisited: overestimating the manifest variability of our actions and appearance. *Journal of Experimental Social Psychology* 38 (1): 93–99.

40. Gilbert, P. (2001). Evolution and social anxiety: the role of attraction, social competition, and social hierarchies. *Psychiatric Clinics* 24 (4): 723–751.

41. O'Day, E.B. and Heimberg, R.G. (2021). Social media use, social anxiety, and loneliness: a systematic review. *Computers in Human Behavior Reports* 3: 100070.

42. London Assembly. (2019). Gender Breakdown of Gangs Matrix (19 December).

43. Knickmeyer, R.C. and Baron-Cohen, S. (2006). Fetal testosterone and sex differences. *Early Human Development* 82 (12): 755–760.

44. Kokštejn, J., Musálek, M., and Tufano, J.J. (2017). Are sex differences in fundamental motor skills uniform throughout the entire preschool period? *PLoS One* 12 (4): e0176556.

45. Kretschmer, L., Salali, G.D., Andersen, L.B. et al. (2023). Gender differences in the distribution of children's physical activity: evidence from nine countries. *International Journal of Behavioral Nutrition and Physical Activity* 20 (1): 103.

46. Leaper, C. (2005). Parenting girls and boys. *Handbook of Parenting* 1: 189–225.

47. Chen, I., Wang, X., Sun, Z. et al. (2024). Intergenerational transmission of parental child-rearing gender-role attitudes and its influence on gender roles in single-parent families. *BMC Psychology* 12 (1): 96.

48. Hanish, L.D. and Fabes, R.A. (2014). Peer socialization of gender in young boys and girls. *Encyclopedia on Early Childhood Development*, 1–4.

49. Davis, J.T. and Hines, M. (2020). How large are gender differences in toy preferences? A systematic review and meta-analysis of toy preference research. *Archives of Sexual Behavior* 49 (2): 373–394.

50. Hassett, J.M., Siebert, E.R., and Wallen, K. (2008). Sex differences in rhesus monkey toy preferences parallel those of children. *Hormones and Behavior* 54 (3): 359–364.

51. Urban, R.J. (1999). Effects of testosterone and growth hormone on muscle function. *The Journal of Laboratory and Clinical Medicine* 134 (1): 7–10.

52. Sjöqvist, F., Garle, M., and Rane, A. (2008). Use of doping agents, particularly anabolic steroids, in sports and society. *The Lancet* 371 (9627): 1872–1882.

53. van Amsterdam, J., Opperhuizen, A., and Hartgens, F. (2010). Adverse health effects of anabolic–androgenic steroids. *Regulatory Toxicology and Pharmacology* 57 (1): 117–123.

54. Eisenegger, C., Kumsta, R., Naef, M. et al. (2017). Testosterone and androgen receptor gene polymorphism are associated with confidence and competitiveness in men. *Hormones and Behavior* 92: 93–102.

55. Vermeer, A.L., Riečanský, I., and Eisenegger, C. (2016). Competition, testosterone, and adult neurobehavioral plasticity. *Progress in Brain Research* 229: 213–238.

56. Kutlikova, H.H., Geniole, S.N., Eisenegger, C. et al. (2021). Not giving up: testosterone promotes persistence against a stronger opponent. *Psychoneuroendocrinology* 128: 105214.

57. Wu, Y., Ou, J., Wang, X. et al. (2022). Exogeneous testosterone increases sexual impulsivity in heterosexual men. *Psychoneuroendocrinology* 145: 105914.

58. Batrinos, M.L. (2012). Testosterone and aggressive behavior in man. *International Journal of Endocrinology and Metabolism* 10 (3): 563.

59. Shores, M.M., Moceri, V.M., Sloan, K.L. et al. (2005). Low testosterone levels predict incident depressive illness in older men: effects of age and medical morbidity. *The Journal of Clinical Psychiatry* 66 (1): 7–14.

60. Yassin, A.A. and Doros, G. (2013). Testosterone therapy in hypogonadal men results in sustained and clinically meaningful weight loss. *Clinical Obesity* 3 (3–4): 73–83.

61. Hsu, Y. and Sun, L. (2010). Factors associated with aggressive responses in pet dogs. *Applied Animal Behaviour Science* 123 (3–4): 108–123.

62. Duke, S.A., Balzer, B.W., and Steinbeck, K.S. (2014). Testosterone and its effects on human male adolescent mood and behavior: a systematic review. *Journal of Adolescent Health* 55 (3): 315–322.

63. Vermeer, A.L., Krol, I., Gausterer, C. et al. (2020). Exogenous testosterone increases status-seeking motivation in men with unstable low social status. *Psychoneuroendocrinology* 113: 104552.

64. Mazur, A. and Booth, A. (1998). Testosterone and dominance in men. *The Behavioral and Brain Sciences* 21 (3): 353–363.

65. Oxford, J., Ponzi, D., and Geary, D.C. (2010). Hormonal responses differ when playing violent video games against an ingroup and outgroup. *Evolution and Human Behavior* 31 (3): 201–209.

66. Bernhardt, P.C., Dabbs, J.M. Jr., Fielden, J.A., and Lutter, C.D. (1998). Testosterone changes during vicarious experiences of winning and losing among fans at sporting events. *Physiology & Behavior* 65 (1): 59–62.

67. Deaner, R.O., Balish, S.M., and Lombardo, M.P. (2016). Sex differences in sports interest and motivation: an evolutionary perspective. *Evolutionary Behavioral Sciences* 10 (2): 73.

68. Cheng, J.T., Kornienko, O., and Granger, D.A. (2018). Prestige in a large-scale social group predicts longitudinal changes in testosterone. *Journal of Personality and Social Psychology* 114 (6): 924.

69. Rochat, M.J. (2023). Sex and gender differences in the development of empathy. *Journal of Neuroscience Research* 101 (5): 718–729.

70. Fisher, H. (2025). Why do men seem more forgetful and women never forget? https://helenfisher.com/why-do-men-seem-more-forgetful-and-women-never-forget-2/

71. Batanova, M. and Loukas, A. (2014). Unique and interactive effects of empathy, family, and school factors on early adolescents' aggression. *Journal of Youth and Adolescence* 43: 1890–1902.

72. Vaillancourt, T. and Krems, J.A. (2018). An evolutionary psychological perspective of indirect aggression. In: *The Development of Relational Aggression* (ed. S.M. Coyne and J.M. Ostrov), 111. Oxford: Oxford University Press.

73. Kile, M. (2024). What the Hell Is Testosterone-Maxxing and Why Are Gym Bros Doing It? *Vice.* (24 December).

74. Salamon, M. (2023). A muscle-building obsession in boys: What to know and do. *Harvard Health Publishing.* (12 May).

75. Fisher, J. (2024). Lifestyle strategies to help prevent natural age-related decline in testosterone. *Harvard Health Publishing.* (13 August).

76. Miguez, M.J., Bueno, D., and Perez, C. (2020). Disparities in sleep health among adolescents: the role of sex, age, and migration. *Sleep Disorders* 2020 (1): 5316364.

77. Guthold, R., Stevens, G.A., Riley, L.M., and Bull, F.C. (2020). Global trends in insufficient physical activity among adolescents: a pooled analysis of 298 population-based surveys with 1· 6 million participants. *The Lancet Child & Adolescent Health* 4 (1): 23–35.

78. Ducharme, J. (2024). Your Brain Doesn't Want You to Exercise. *Time* (30 January).

79. Luders, E. and Kurth, F. (2020). Structural differences between male and female brains. *Handbook of Clinical Neurology* 175: 3–11.

80. Eriksson, M., Marschik, P.B., Tulviste, T. et al. (2012). Differences between girls and boys in emerging language skills: evidence from 10 language communities. *British Journal of Developmental Psychology* 30 (2): 326–343.

81. McBurney, D.H., Gaulin, S.J.C., Devineni, T., and Adams, C. (1997). Superior spatial memory of women: stronger evidence for the gathering hypothesis. *Evolution and Human Behavior* 18 (3): 165–174.

82. Yuan, L., Kong, F., Luo, Y. et al. (2019). Gender differences in large-scale and small-scale spatial ability: a systematic review based on behavioral and neuroimaging research. *Frontiers in Behavioral Neuroscience* 13: 128.

83. Lenroot, R.K. and Giedd, J.N. (2010). Sex differences in the adolescent brain. *Brain and Cognition* 72 (1): 46–55.

84. Demarin, V. and Morović, S. (2014). Neuroplasticity. *Periodicum Biologorum* 116 (2): 209–211.

85. Crowley, S.J., Acebo, C., and Carskadon, M.A. (2007). Sleep, circadian rhythms, and delayed phase in adolescence. *Sleep Medicine* 8 (6): 602–612.

86. Tang, N.K., Fiecas, M., Afolalu, E.F., and Wolke, D. (2017). Changes in sleep duration, quality, and medication use are prospectively associated with health and wellbeing: analysis of the UK household longitudinal study. *Sleep* 40 (3): https://doi.org/10.1093/sleep/zsw079.

87. Adriatico, J.M., Cruz, A., Tiong, R.C., and Racho-Sabugo, C.R. (2022). An analysis on the impact of choice overload to consumer decision paralysis. *Journal of Economics, Finance and Accounting Studies* 4 (1): 55–75.

88. Cheval, B., Tipura, E., Burra, N. et al. (2018). Avoiding sedentary behaviors requires more cortical resources than avoiding physical activity: an EEG study. *Neuropsychologia* 119: 68–80.

89. Rideout, V., Peebles, A., Mann, S., and Robb, M. (2021). *The Common Sense Census: Media Use by Tweens and Teens*. San Francisco, CA: Common Sense.

90. DeAngelis, T. (2024). Teens are spending nearly 5 hours daily on social media. Here are the mental health outcomes. *American Psychological Association* 55 (3): 80.

91. Fleming, A. (2024). Only 3% of UK 12-year-olds don't have a smartphone. Here is how four of them feel about it. *The Guardian* (23 September).

92. Iwase, T., Yoshida, M., and Hashizume, Y. (2015). Factors contributing to improve the quality of life in dementia-free centenarians. *Journal of the Neurological Sciences* 357: e129.

93. Al-Samarraie, H., Bello, K., Alzahrani, A.I. et al. (2022). Young users' social media addiction: causes, consequences and preventions. *Information Technology & People* 35 (7): 2314–2343.

94. Haidt, J. (2024). *The Anxious Generation: How the Great Rewiring of Childhood is Causing an Epidemic of Mental Illness*. London: Penguin.

95. Khouja, J.N., Munafò, M.R., Tilling, K. et al. (2019). Is screen time associated with anxiety or depression in young people? Results from a UK birth cohort. *BMC Public Health* 19: 1–11.

96. Maras, D., Flament, M.F., Murray, M. et al. (2015). Screen time is associated with depression and anxiety in Canadian youth. *Preventive Medicine* 73: 133–138.

97. Nguyen, N.D., Truong, N., Dao, P.Q., and Nguyen, H.H. (2025). Can online behaviors be linked to mental health? Active versus passive social network usage on depression via envy and self-esteem. *Computers in Human Behavior* 162: 108455.

98. Martingano, A.J., Konrath, S., Zarins, S., and Okaomee, A.A. (2022). Empathy, narcissism, alexithymia, and social media use. *Psychology of Popular Media* 11 (4): 413.

99. Hoxhaj, B., Xhani, D., Kapo, S., and Sinaj, E. (2023). The role of social media on self-image and self-esteem: a study on Albanian teenagers. *Journal of Educational and Social Research* 13.

100. Alonzo, R., Hussain, J., Stranges, S., and Anderson, K.K. (2021). Interplay between social media use, sleep quality, and mental health in youth: a systematic review. *Sleep Medicine Reviews* 56: 101414.

101. Wolfers, L.N. and Utz, S. (2022). Social media use, stress, and coping. *Current Opinion in Psychology* 45: 101305.

102. Yang, H., Zhang, S., Diao, Z., and Sun, D. (2023). What motivates users to continue using current short video applications? A dual-path examination of flow experience and cognitive lock-in. *Telematics and Informatics* 85: 102050.

103. Pellegrino, A., Abe, M., and Shannon, R. (2022). The dark side of social media: content effects on the relationship between materialism and consumption behaviors. *Frontiers in Psychology* 13: 870614.

104. Luo, M. and Hancock, J.T. (2020). Modified self-praise in social media: Humblebragging, self-presentation, and perceptions of (in) sincerity. In: *Complimenting Behavior and (Self-) Praise Across Social Media* (ed. M.E. Placencia and Z.R. Eslami), 289–310. Amsterdam: John Benjamins Publishing Company.

105. Courtright, J. and Caplan, S. (2020). A meta-analysis of mobile phone use and presence. *Human Communication & Technology* 1 (2): 20–35.

106. Lembke, A. (2021). *Dopamine Nation: Finding Balance in the Age of Indulgence*. London: Penguin.

107. Cristol, H., Mitchell, K., and McPhillips, A. (2024). Dopamine: What It Is & What It Does. *WebMD*. (09 July).

108. Firth, J., Torous, J., Stubbs, B. et al. (2019). The "online brain": how the Internet may be changing our cognition. *World Psychiatry* 18 (2): 119–129.

109. Flannery, J.S., Burnell, K., Kwon, S. et al. (2024). Developmental changes in brain function linked with addiction-like social media use two years later. *Social Cognitive and Affective Neuroscience* 19 (1): nsae008.

110. Fuhrmann, D., Knoll, L.J., and Blakemore, S. (2015). Adolescence as a sensitive period of brain development. *Trends in Cognitive Sciences (Regul Ed)* 19 (10): 558–566.

111. Bhargava, V.R. and Velasquez, M. (2021). Ethics of the attention economy: the problem of social media addiction. *Business Ethics Quarterly* 31 (3): 321–359.

112. Hart, J. (2023). Harvard study of adult development: human connection is key to health and wellbeing. *Integrative and Complementary Therapies* 29 (3): 122–124.

113. Dunbar, R. (2021). *Friends: Understanding the Power of Our Most Important Relationships*. New York, Hachette.

114. Radesky, J., Weeks, H., Schaller, A., Robb, M., Mann, S., and Lenhart, A. (2023). *Constant Companion: A Week in the Life of a Young Person's Smartphone Use* (26 September). San Francisco, CA: Common Sense.

115. Ross, C. (2011). How technology is turning us into faster talkers. *CBC News* (31 October).

116. Salazar-Miranda, A., Fan, Z., Baick, M.B., et al. (2024). *Shifting Patterns of Social Interaction: Exploring the Social Life of Urban Spaces Through AI*. Working Paper Series 33185. National Bureau of Economic Research.

117. Hsieh, S. and Liu, L. (2005). The nature of switch cost: task set configuration or carry-over effect? *Cognitive Brain Research* 22 (2): 165–175.

118. May, K.E. and Elder, A.D. (2018). Efficient, helpful, or distracting? A literature review of media multitasking in relation to academic performance. *International Journal of Educational Technology in Higher Education* 15 (1): 1–17.

119. Barks, A., Searight, H.R., and Ratwik, S. (2011). Effects of text messaging on academic performance. *Signum Temporis* 4 (1): 4.

120. Mujica, A.L., Crowell, C.R., Villano, M.A., and Uddin, K.M. (2022). Addiction by design: some dimensions and challenges of excessive social media use. *Medical Research Archives* 10 (2): https://doi.org/10.18103/mra.v10i2.2677.

121. Hale, L., Kirschen, G.W., LeBourgeois, M.K. et al. (2018). Youth screen media habits and sleep: sleep-friendly screen behavior recommendations for clinicians, educators, and parents. *Child and Adolescent Psychiatric Clinics of North America* 27 (2): 229–245.

122. Kent, J. (2023). Need a Break from Social Media? Here's Why You Should — and How to Do It. *Harvard Summer School*. (08 May).

123. Terrier, L., Lévêque, M., and Amelot, A. (2019). Brain lobotomy: a historical and moral dilemma with no alternative? *World Neurosurgery* 132: 211–218.

124. Zheng, H. and Echave, P. (2021). Are recent cohorts getting worse? Trends in US adult physiological status, mental health, and health behaviors across a century of birth cohorts. *American Journal of Epidemiology* 190 (11): 2242–2255.

125. Department for Work and Pensions. (2025). New survey suggests benefits system is letting down people with mental health conditions who want to work (06 February). https://www.gov.uk/government/publications/work-aspirations-and-support-needs-of-health-and-disability-customers

126. Lacocque, P. (1982). Desacralizing life and its mystery: the Jonah complex revisited. *Journal of Psychology and Theology* 10 (2): 113–119.

127. Huggett, R. (2002). *Geoecology: An Evolutionary Approach*. Abingdon: Routledge.

128. Kennon, J. (2016). Pornography Study Failed After Researchers Couldn't Find a Single Man Who Hadn't Viewed X-Rated Material (11 August).

129. Black, J., Green, A., and Rickards, T. (1998). *Gods, Demons and Symbols of Ancient Mesopotamia: An Illustrated Dictionary*. London: British Museum Press.

130. Abel, R. (2004). *Encyclopedia of early cinema*. Abingdon: Routledge.

131. Kutchinsky, B. (1970). Pornography in Denmark. Technical Reports of the Commission on Obscenity and Pornography. 4th Edition. *The Marketplace: Empirical Studies. 263*.

132. Feldman, R.S. (2009). *Discovering the Life Span*. Chennai: Pearson Education India.

133. De Waal, F.B. (1995). Bonobo sex and society. *Scientific American* 272 (3): 82–88.

134. Chakrabarti, S. and Jhala, Y.V. (2019). Battle of the sexes: a multi-male mating strategy helps lionesses win the gender war of fitness. *Behavioral Ecology* 30 (4): 1050–1061.

135. Snyder, R.J., Lawson, D.P., Zhang, A. et al. (2004). Reproduction in giant pandas. In: *Giant Pandas: Biology and Conservation* (ed. D.G. Lindburg and K. Baragona), 125–132. Berkeley: University of California Press.

136. Hilton, D.L. Jr. and Watts, C. (2011). Pornography addiction: a neuroscience perspective. *Surgical Neurology International* 2: 19.

137. Sabatinelli, D., Bradley, M.M., Lang, P.J. et al. (2007). Pleasure rather than salience activates human nucleus accumbens and medial prefrontal cortex. *Journal of Neurophysiology* 98 (3): 1374–1379.

138. Di Chiara, G. (2002). Nucleus accumbens shell and core dopamine: differential role in behavior and addiction. *Behavioural Brain Research* 137 (1–2): 75–114.

139. Wilson, G. and Jack, A. (2017). *Your Brain on Porn: Internet Pornography and the Emerging Science of Addiction*. Margate: Commonwealth Publishing Kent.

140. Guitart-Masip, M., Bunzeck, N., Stephan, K.E. et al. (2010). Contextual novelty changes reward representations in the striatum. *Journal of Neuroscience* 30 (5): 1721–1726.

141. Love, T., Laier, C., Brand, M. et al. (2015). Neuroscience of internet pornography addiction: a review and update. *Behavioral Science* 5 (3): 388–433.

142. Jacobs, T., Geysemans, B., Van Hal, G. et al. (2021). Associations between online pornography consumption and sexual dysfunction in young men: multivariate analysis based on an international web-based survey. *JMIR Public Health and Surveillance* 7 (10): e32542.

143. Begovic, H. (2019). Pornography induced erectile dysfunction among young men. *Dignity: A Journal of Analysis of Exploitation and Violence* 4 (1): 5.

144. Luscombe, B. (2016). Porn and the threat to virility. *Time* 187: 40–47.

145. Thomas, M.S. (2012). Brain plasticity and education. *British Journal of Educational Psychology-Monograph Series II: Educational Neuroscience* 8: 142–156.

146. Ogden, A. (2021). *Life and Times of Lieutenant General Adrian Carton de Wiart*. London: Bloomsbury.

147. Hernon, I. (2016). *Britain's Forgotten Wars: Colonial Campaigns of the 19th Century*. Cheltenham: The History Press.

148. Hollis, P. (2024). *Liechtenstein's 81st soldier*. https://pjhollis123.medium.com/liechtensteins-81st-soldier-2e4d3e85fcb3.

149. Clodfelter, M. (2017). *Warfare and Armed Conflicts: A Statistical Encyclopedia of Casualty and Other Figures, 1492-2015*. Jefferson: McFarland.

150. Luckhurst, T. (2019). Honduras v El Salvador: The football match that kicked off a war. *BBC* (27 June).

151. Lahti, E.E. (2019). Embodied fortitude: an introduction to the Finnish construct of sisu. *International Journal of Wellbeing* 9 (1): https://doi.org/10.5502/ijw.v9i1.672.

152. Pearson, J.C., Lemons, D., and McGinnis, W. (2005). Modulating Hox gene functions during animal body patterning. *Nature Reviews Genetics* 6 (12): 893–904.

153. Krumlauf, R. (1994). Hox genes in vertebrate development. *Cell* 78 (2): 191–201.

154. Kolb, B., Mychasiuk, R., Muhammad, A. et al. (2012). Experience and the developing prefrontal cortex. *Proceedings of the National Academy of Sciences* 109 (supplement_2): 17186–17193.

155. Verhaak, P.F. (1997). Somatic disease and psychological disorder. *Journal of Psychosomatic Research* 42 (3): 261–273.

156. Tabak, B.A., McCullough, M.E., Szeto, A. et al. (2011). Oxytocin indexes relational distress following interpersonal harms in women. *Psychoneuroendocrinology* 36 (1): 115–122.

157. Olff, M., Frijling, J.L., Kubzansky, L.D. et al. (2013). The role of oxytocin in social bonding, stress regulation and mental health: an update on the moderating effects of context and interindividual differences. *Psychoneuroendocrinology* 38 (9): 1883–1894.

158. Wirobski, G., Crockford, C., Deschner, T., and Neumann, I.D. (2024). Oxytocin and cortisol concentrations in urine and saliva in response to physical exercise in humans. *Psychoneuroendocrinology* 168: 107144.

159. Griffin, J.W., Bauer, R., and Scherf, K.S. (2021). A quantitative meta-analysis of face recognition deficits in autism: 40 years of research. *Psychological Bulletin* 147 (3): 268.

160. Baron-Cohen, S., Ashwin, E., Ashwin, C. et al. (2009). Talent in autism: hyper-systemizing, hyper-attention to detail and sensory hypersensitivity. *Philosophical Transactions of the Royal Society, B: Biological Sciences* 364 (1522): 1377–1383.

161. Taylor, H. and Vestergaard, M.D. (2022). Developmental dyslexia: disorder or specialization in exploration? *Frontiers in Psychology* 13: 889245.

162. Hattenstone, S. (2021). Greta Thunberg has spent three years raising the alarm on the climate crisis. *The Guardian* (25 September).

163. Respers France, L. (2022). Billie Eilish finds having Tourette's syndrome 'exhausting'. *CNN* (23 May).

164. Banfield-Mwachi, M. (2023). David Beckham reveals impact of OCD in new documentary. *The Guardian* (28 April).

165. Doyle, N. (2019). Richard Branson Opens Door To Bigger Thinking On Neurodiversity. *Forbes* (22 October).

166. Chapman, G. (2016). Autism a Silicon Valley asset with social quirks. *Phys. org.* (28 August).

167. Duhigg, C. (2013). *The Power of Habit: Why We Do What We Do and How to Change*. New York: Random House.

168. Blocken, B., van Druenen, T., Toparlar, Y. et al. (2018). Aerodynamic drag in cycling pelotons: new insights by CFD simulation and wind tunnel testing. *Journal of Wind Engineering and Industrial Aerodynamics* 179: 319–337.

169. Eichhorn, L. (2024). Freediving–from Tradition to Modernity. *Dtsch Z Sportmed* 75: 205–206.

170. Fava, G.A. and Guidi, J. (2020). The pursuit of euthymia. *World Psychiatry* 19 (1): 40–50.

171. Dweck, C.S. (2009). Mindsets: developing talent through a growth mindset. *Olympic Coach* 21 (1): 4–7.

172. Duckworth, A.L., Eichstaedt, J.C., and Ungar, L.H. (2015). The mechanics of human achievement. *Social and Personality Psychology Compass* 9 (7): 359–369.

Index

ALSO AVAILABLE BY
ANDY COPE

9780857089397
**The Art of Being
A Brilliant Teenager**

9780857088574
**A Girl's Guide
to Being Fearless**

9780857087867
Diary of a Brilliant Kid

9780857088918
Brill Kid - The Big Number 2

AVAILABLE WHEREVER
BOOKS ARE SOLD

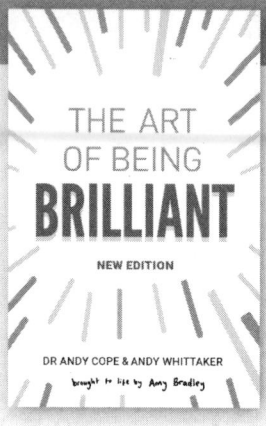